UPDATED EDITION

Online Audio
Included

# EASY
# ADULT PIANO
## BEGINNER'S COURSE
### A Step-By-Step Learning System

**PLAYBACK+**
*Speed • Pitch • Balance • Loop*

To access audio, visit:
**www.halleonard.com/mylibrary**
Enter Code
5045-6776-5295-9872

ISBN 978-1-5400-4128-9

**HAL•LEONARD®**

E-Z Play ® TODAY Music Notation © 1975 HAL LEONARD LLC
E-Z PLAY and EASY ELECTRONIC KEYBOARD MUSIC are registered trademarks of HAL LEONARD LLC.

Visit Hal Leonard Online at
**www.halleonard.com**

Contact us:
**Hal Leonard**
7777 West Bluemound Road
Milwaukee, WI 53213
Email: info@halleonard.com

In Europe, contact:
**Hal Leonard Europe Limited**
42 Wigmore Street
Marylebone, London, W1U 2RN
Email: info@halleonardeurope.com

In Australia, contact:
**Hal Leonard Australia Pty. Ltd.**
4 Lentara Court
Cheltenham, Victoria, 3192 Australia
Email: info@halleonard.com.au

# INTRODUCTION

Welcome to the **Easy Adult Piano Beginner's Course**, a three-part method that will show you how to make music at the piano and have a lot of fun doing it. How? By using familiar songs supported by easy-to-understand instruction, simple examples, and related exercises.

In no time at all, using Notes-That-Name-Themselves, you'll be performing many of the tunes you've always wanted to play.

**PART 1** introduces the fundamentals of music and enough keyboard technique to help anyone play songs, using Easy Beginner arrangements.

**PART 2** prepares you to move on to a higher level of playing, using Easy Pro arrangements.

**PART 3** is a special supplement containing additional songs for you to enjoy while learning Parts 1 and 2.

# CONTENTS

# Introducing the Keyboard

Playing is probably a lot easier than you think. The following examples will help you get started.

A-B-C key stickers are enclosed to help you match the notes on the music with the correct keys on the keyboard. Place them as shown on the illustration. Start with the C key that's beneath the brand-name of the piano. (See page 5 for the location of Middle C.)

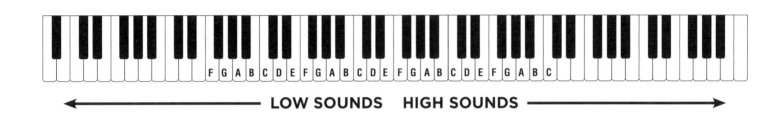

There are high and low sounds on the piano. High sounds are found to the right, going up the keyboard. Low sounds are found to the left, going down the keyboard. Try this on your piano.

A keyboard is comprised of black and white keys. The black keys are in groups of two and three and will help you locate the various white keys.

## MIDDLE C

The first step to playing the piano is to locate the key called Middle C, because it's the main point of reference on your keyboard. Think of it as "home base."

Start by locating the two-black-key group nearest the middle of your keyboard, usually beneath the brand name of the piano. The white key just to the left is Middle C. In our examples on this page, Middle C is shaded gray.

The three-black-key group can be used to locate the white key called F, just to the left. By knowing where the C and F keys are, you can easily locate the rest of the musical alphabet.

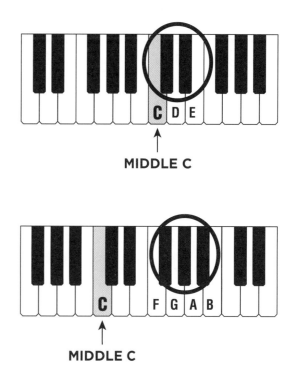

## THE MUSICAL ALPHABET

Seven letters make up the musical alphabet: A, B, C, D, E, F, G. These seven letters repeat over and over to name all the white keys on the piano. Your keyboard guide shows enough of these letters and notes to get you started.

While there is only one key called Middle C, there are many other Cs on the keyboard. Use the two- and three-black-key groups as a guide to locate any letter of the musical alphabet.

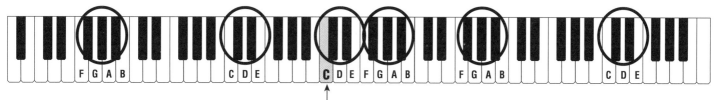

## THE GRAND STAFF

Piano music is written on lines and spaces. A *grand staff* is two staffs, each of five lines and four spaces, joined by a bracket.

The *treble clef* 𝄞 appears at the beginning of the upper staff; the notes that follow are usually played with your right hand. The *bass clef* 𝄢 appears at the beginning of the lower staff; the notes that follow are usually played with your left hand.

*Middle C* falls in between the treble and bass clefs – hence its name – and is often played by either hand. Coincidentally, on your piano this is the C-key closest to the middle of the keyboard.

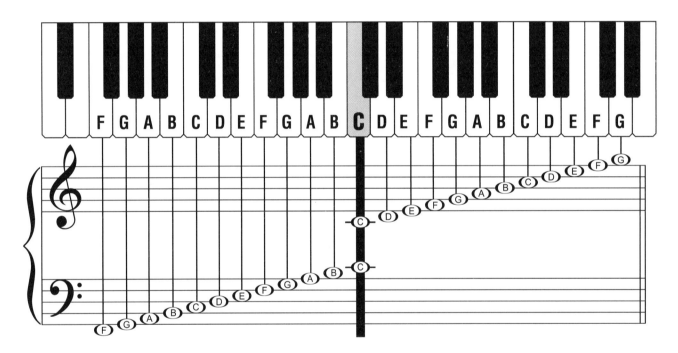

**MIDDLE C**

# When the Saints Go Marching In

## PLAYING A MELODY

With your right hand, play the first five keys one at a time, starting with your thumb on Middle C: C-D-E-F-G.

The illustrations on this page show finger numbers, with each hand numbered 1 through 5, starting with the thumb. Not only are suggested fingerings helpful in this beginning stage, they'll also aid you later as the music becomes more involved. For now, at least, it's recommended that you observe all suggested fingerings.

Do the same with your left hand, starting at the next C-key to the left of Middle C.

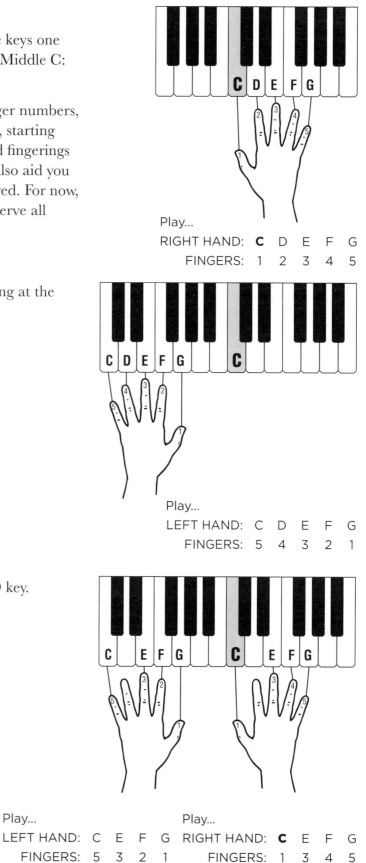

Play...

| RIGHT HAND: | C | D | E | F | G |
|---|---|---|---|---|---|
| FINGERS: | 1 | 2 | 3 | 4 | 5 |

Play...

| LEFT HAND: | C | D | E | F | G |
|---|---|---|---|---|---|
| FINGERS: | 5 | 4 | 3 | 2 | 1 |

Now, repeat. This time, leave out the D key. Start with one hand, then the other.

Play...

| LEFT HAND: | C | E | F | G |
|---|---|---|---|---|
| FINGERS: | 5 | 3 | 2 | 1 |

Play...

| RIGHT HAND: | C | E | F | G |
|---|---|---|---|---|
| FINGERS: | 1 | 3 | 4 | 5 |

Sound familiar? You've just played the first part of "When the Saints Go Marching In"!

# WHEN THE SAINTS GO MARCHING IN

*Match the letter in the notes on the staff to the letters on your keyboard guide – and play!*

Words by Katherine E. Purvis
Music by James M. Black

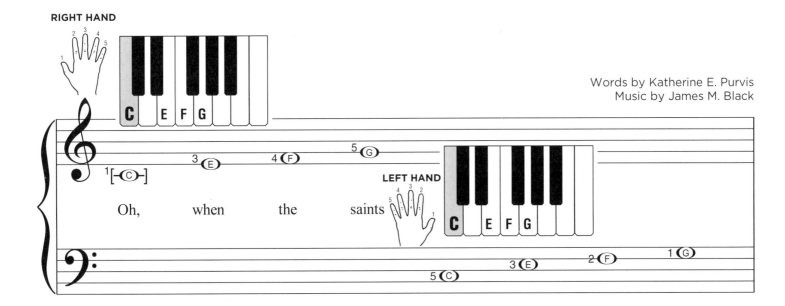

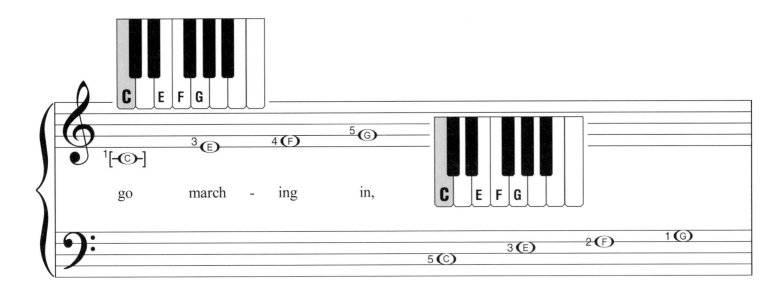

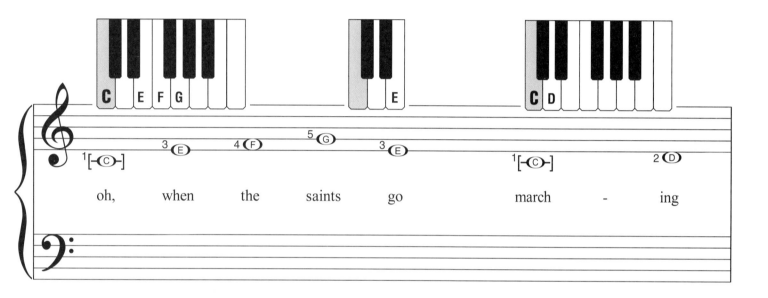

oh,       when       the       saints       go       march  -       ing

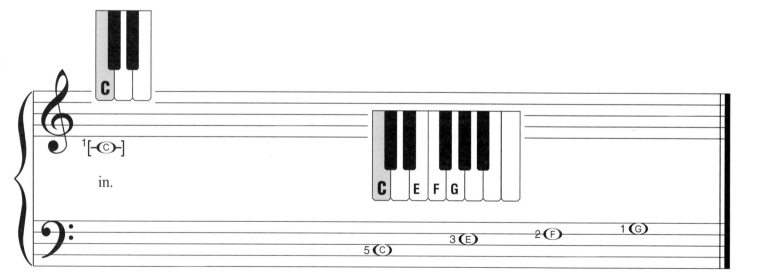

in.

# Chopsticks

## BEATS AND HOW TO COUNT THEM

In music, time is measured in *beats*. To help you understand what beats are, tap your foot in a steady, even manner. Each complete down-and-up motion equals one beat. To keep track of the beats, a number is counted each time your foot taps the floor.

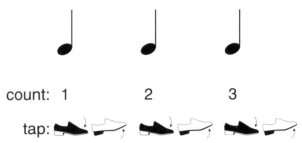

"Chopsticks" consists entirely of *quarter notes*, each of which is worth *one beat*.

Beats grouped together make up certain rhythms. A waltz is a rhythm where beats occur in groups of three. How many times have you heard the phrase "oom-pah-pah"? "Chopsticks" is a waltz. To help show beats in groups of three, *bar lines* are used to divide the staff into *measures*. A waltz has three beats in each measure, as shown by the 3 in the example.

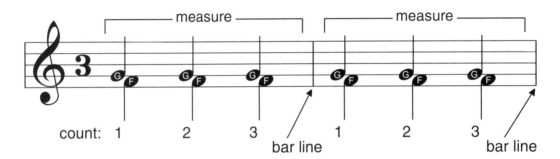

For ease of reading this song, all notes appear in the treble staff. Notes with stems up ♩ are played with your right hand. Notes with stems down ♩ are played with your left hand. Play each pair of quarter notes at the same time.

Here's your starting hand position. Use the index fingers of both hands throughout the song.

For your convenience, the measures in each song are numbered; reference numbers appear at the left of each line of music.

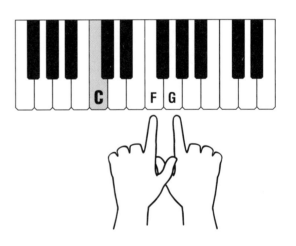

# CHOPSTICKS

By Arthur de Lulli

# Cockles and Mussels

## RHYTHM – BEATS – TIME

Rhythm plays a large part in everyday living; every step you take, each intake of breath – even the cycle of waking and sleeping – is rhythmic. Music is rhythmic, too, and uses symbols as a visual aid. You already know one – the quarter note ♩. Here are two more:

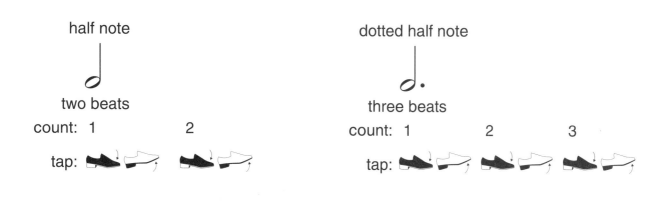

## TIME SIGNATURE

*Time signatures* are used to structure beats into uniform measures. 3/4 is one kind of time signature – the upper number (in this case, 3) tells how many beats occur in each measure. The lower number, 4, tells you the quarter note receives one beat. You'll learn about other kinds of signatures later.

# COCKLES AND MUSSELS

The keyboards shown here will aid your left hand. The gray MIDDLE C key is indicated.

Traditional Irish Folksong

# Row, Row, Row Your Boat

## PLAYING CHORD ACCOMPANIMENT I

Up to now you've played one note with each hand. This song introduces chords, which provide a background for melodies. A *chord* is a combination of three or more keys played at the same time, mostly by your left hand and mostly in the keyboard area to the left of Middle C.

This song uses only the C chord. The illustration shows how it looks on your sheet music and where to play it on your piano. Try it a few times.

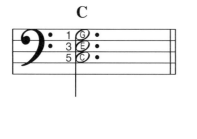

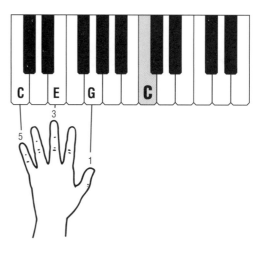

Today's popular sheet music and books also show *chord symbols* above the melody. This letter is a form of shorthand that indicates the name of the accompaniment chord written in the bass staff. Most musicians look at just chord symbols and, from experience, know which notes to play; they don't even look at the bass staff. As you become more proficient at playing chords, you may also want to do the same. Do whatever is easier for you. (You'll find more information on playing chord accompaniment on page 21.)

## TIES

A *tie* is a curved line placed between two or more notes. Ties are used to make longer-sounding tones. The example shown would be played as one note, six beats long. Letters don't appear in notes following ties.

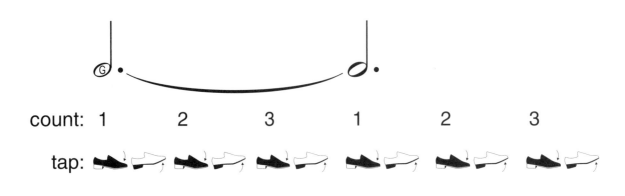

Chords may also be tied. Hold each chord until the next chord symbol appears above the music.

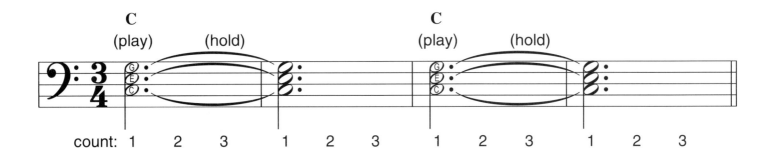

Note: In measures 5 and 6 of the song, your right thumb must cross under your second finger to play the E note.

# ROW, ROW, ROW YOUR BOAT

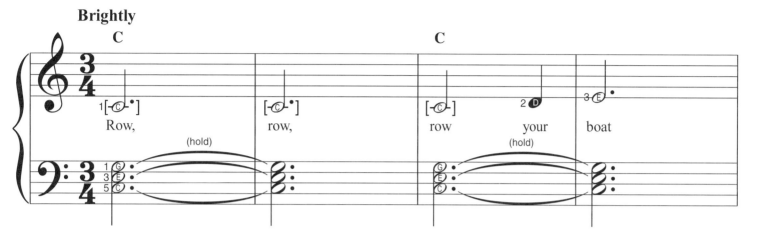

Traditional

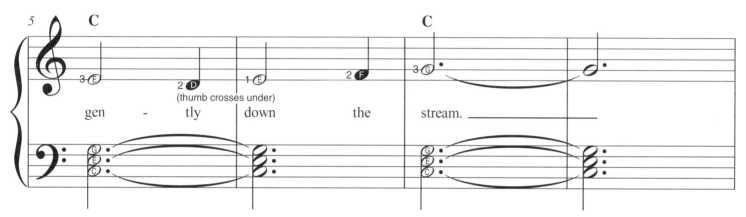

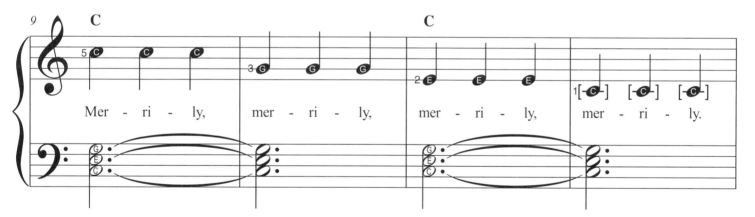

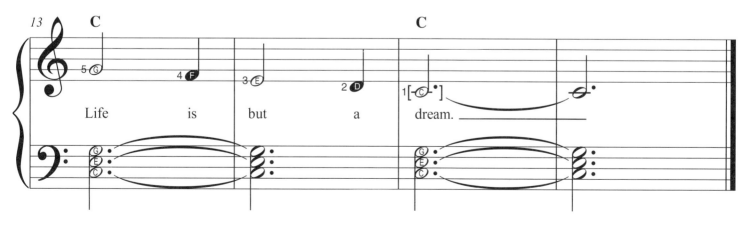

# Review Quiz

## A. MATCHING

Match the numbers in the left-hand column to the correct answers in the right-hand column.

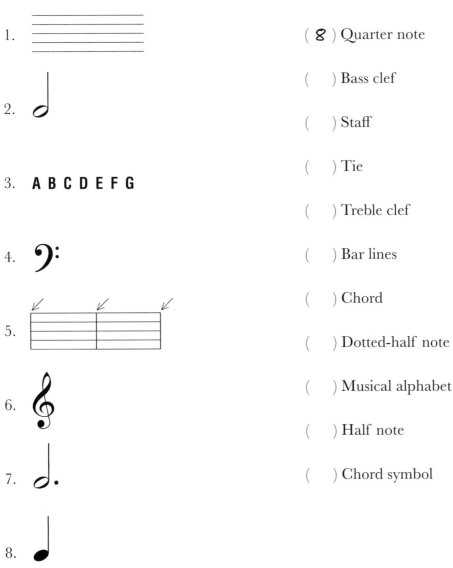

1.

2.

3. **A B C D E F G**

4.

5.

6.

7.

8.

9.

10.

11.

( **8** ) Quarter note

(    ) Bass clef

(    ) Staff

(    ) Tie

(    ) Treble clef

(    ) Bar lines

(    ) Chord

(    ) Dotted-half note

(    ) Musical alphabet

(    ) Half note

(    ) Chord symbol

## B. NAME THE NOTES

Below is the melody of "The Skaters," without the letter names. Write the letter name near each note and then play the melody. Hint: One note is included that you haven't played before. Watch the ties!

## THE SKATERS

Note: A complete arrangement of "The Skaters" appears in the Easy Favorites section of this book. See page 20 for more information.

## OTHER SONGS YOU CAN NOW PLAY...

The Easy Favorites section contains more music you can play as you work your way through this book. Because there are two arrangements of each song – an Easy Beginner and an Easy Pro – you can start right now. With what you've learned up to now, you can play the arrangements shown here by reading the notes appearing for both hands.

## THEME "FROM THE NEW WORLD" SYMPHONY

Easy Beginner

## BEAUTIFUL BROWN EYES

Easy Beginner

At various places in this book, other songs in Easy Favorites are also listed for your playing enjoyment.

# HOME SWEET HOME

## PICK-UP NOTES

*Pick-up notes* are any notes before the first complete measure of a song. The example below has a 3/4 time signature, but the first measure has only two beats; the third beat appears at the end of the song. Incidentally, measure 1 is the first complete measure after the pick-up notes.

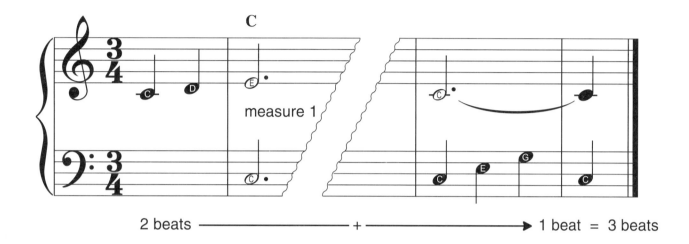

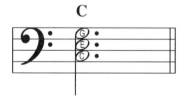

## PLAYING CHORD ACCOMPANIMENT II

As you learned on page 15, a *chord* is a combination of three or more notes played at the same time. You also learned that the C chord is made up of the notes C-E-G. This is called the root position of the chord because the C note is the lowest note.

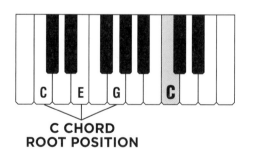

All chords can be played in different positions on the keyboard. For example, the next illustration shows the *1st inversion* of the C chord. It's called an inversion because the C note has been moved to the top of the chord (inverted).

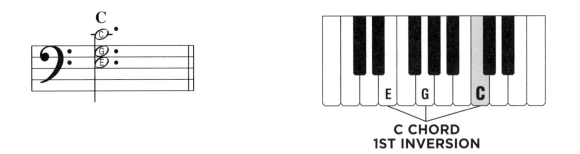

Moving the bottom E note to the top, creates the *2nd inversion* of the C chord.

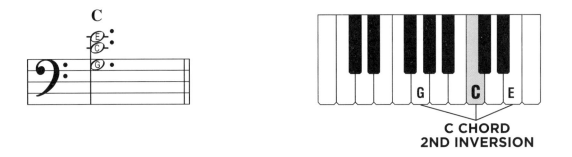

Notice that each position still has the same three note letter names – they're just in a different order.

If you again invert the bottom note of the *2nd inversion*, you create the *root position* (C-E-G), but in a different location on the keyboard.

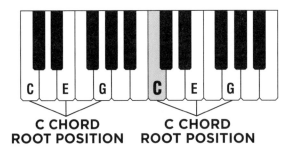

In most cases, the higher *root position* would not be used for an accompaniment chord because melody notes may "bump into" the chord notes.

Each inversion can also be played in a different location on the keyboard. Use the location that doesn't bump into melody notes.

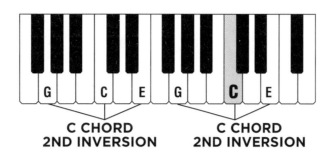

The next song, "Home Sweet Home," uses two additional chords: the F chord and the G chord. The example shows the different positions of each. (Only one location is shown for the 2nd inversions because the higher ones would be too high.)

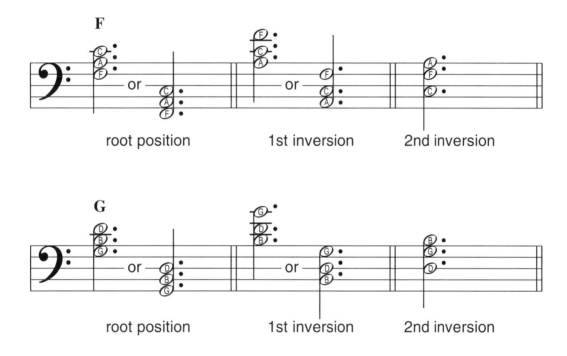

From this point on, chord symbols are shown on all songs should you wish to play a chord accompaniment. A helpful chart showing chords and their inversions is provided on page 40.

## OTHER SONGS YOU CAN NOW PLAY...

Try the Easy Beginner arrangements of "Barcarolle" (page 106) and "Long, Long Ago" (page 108).

# HOME SWEET HOME

Words by John Howard Payne
Music by Henry R. Bishop

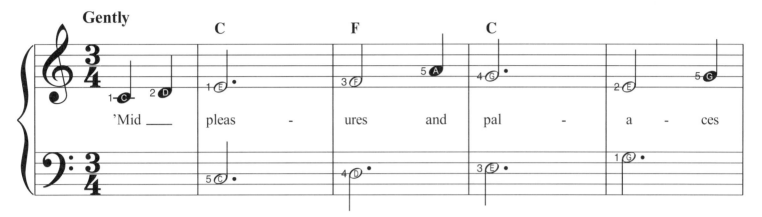

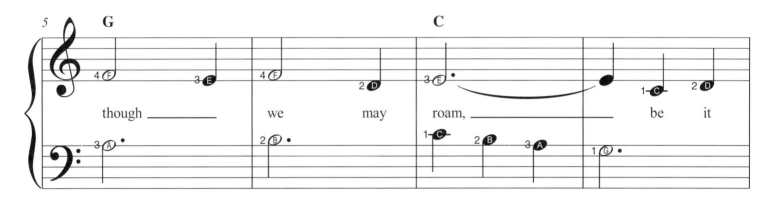

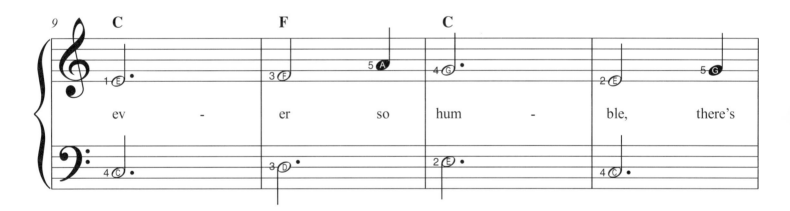

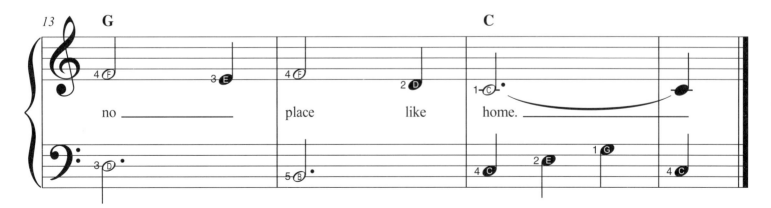

# WHEN THE SAINTS GO MARCHING IN

## TIME SIGNATURE

4/4 is another kind of time signature. The upper number, 4, tells you there are four beats in each measure; the lower 4 tells you the quarter note receives one beat.

## WHOLE NOTE

## THE PEDALS ON YOUR PIANO

At the lower front of your piano, you'll see one, two, or three pedals, depending on the piano model you own.

The pedal farthest to the left (whether there are two or three) is used for playing softly. The middle pedal name and usage varies from one piano model to another; it is not used in this book, so you need not concern yourself with it.

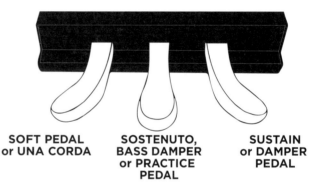

**SOFT PEDAL or UNA CORDA**    **SOSTENUTO, BASS DAMPER or PRACTICE PEDAL**    **SUSTAIN or DAMPER PEDAL**

The one pedal present on all pianos is called the sustain or damper pedal and that's the one you'll use when you play this song.

When you play a note or chord, and at the same time press down this pedal, the musical tone continues to sustain, or linger, long after your fingers have left the keys. When you release the pedal, the sound stops. This can help you create a really big, full sound if you use the pedal properly.

The example shown is from the ending of "When the Saints Go Marching In." Play it without the sustain pedal and then press the pedal and play the example again. You'll really like what you hear!

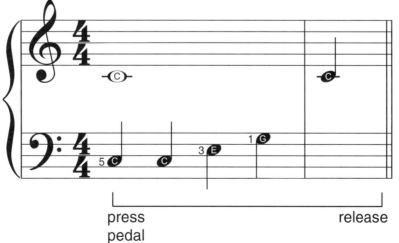

# WHEN THE SAINTS GO MARCHING IN

Words by Katherine E. Purvis
Music by James M. Black

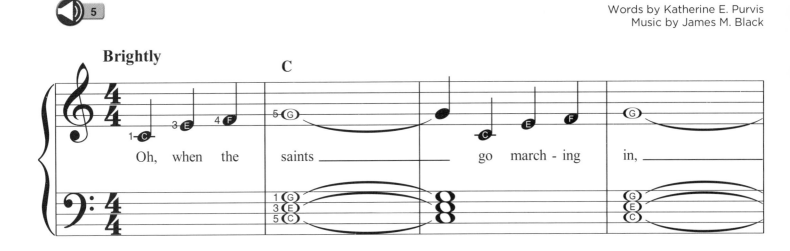

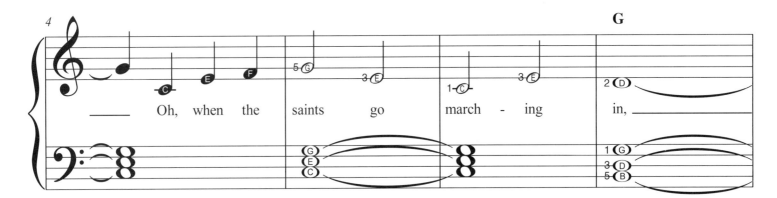

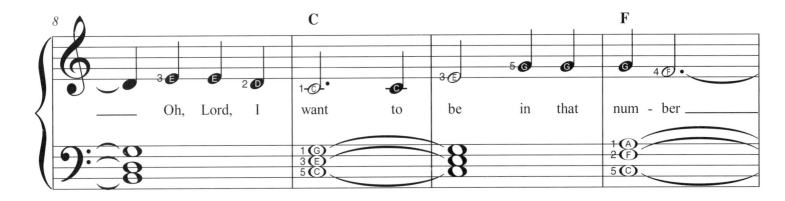

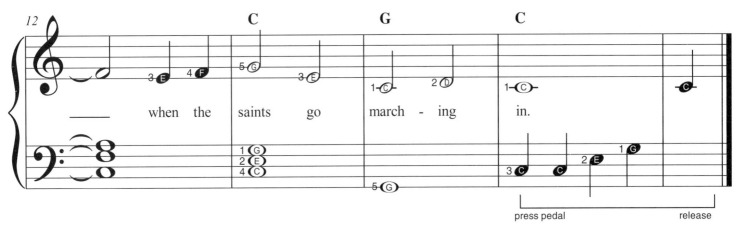

# MAORI FAREWELL SONG

## BROKEN CHORDS

In the last song, you played the notes of the C chord one-at-a-time to create an interesting ending for the arrangement. The same idea can be applied to the accompaniment to add interest and variety to certain places within a song. Here's how it works with the C chord…

Play each note of the chord separately, starting with the lowest note (beat 1), then the middle note (beat 2), and the highest note (beat 3). The technical term for this is *arpeggio*. (We'll discuss this further on page 33.)

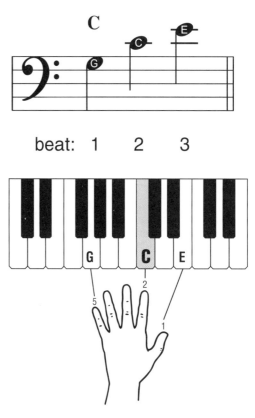

## SHARP ♯

This symbol, called a sharp, appears before a note to indicate a raise in pitch (the sound of the note). To locate D♯, first find D on the keyboard. D♯ is the very next key to the right. It's a black key. Any sharp key is the one immediately to the right, whether black or white.

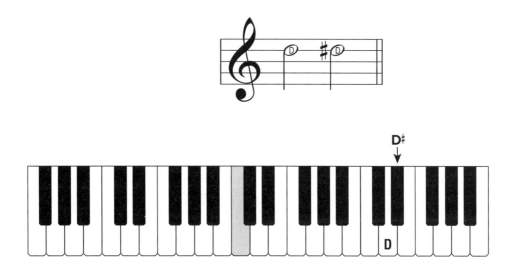

# MAORI FAREWELL SONG

Traditional New Zealand Folksong

**Moderately**

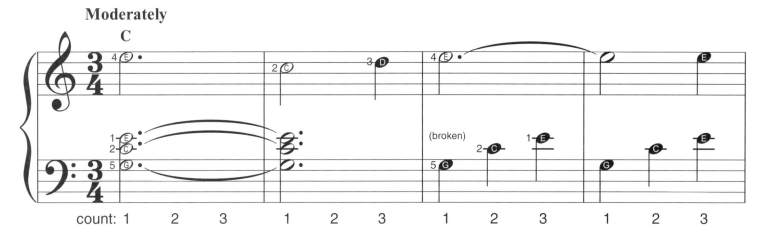

count: 1    2    3    1    2    3    1    2    3    1    2    3

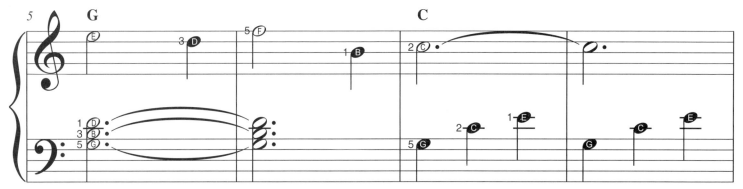

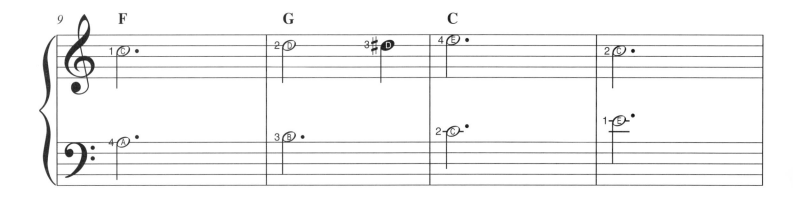

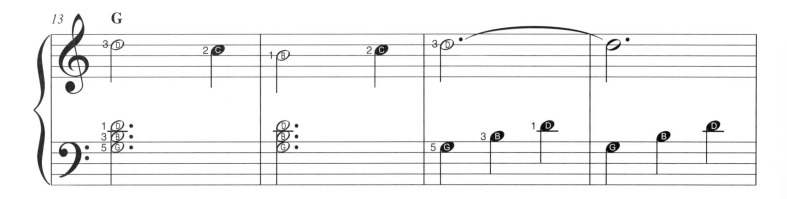

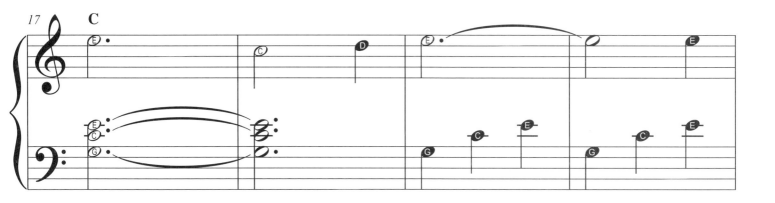

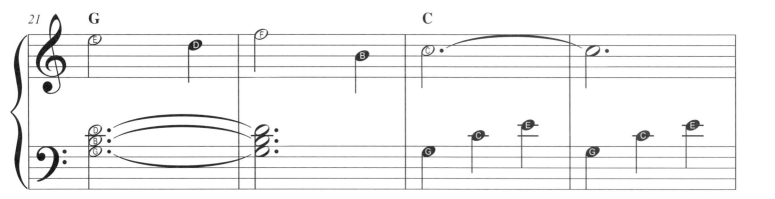

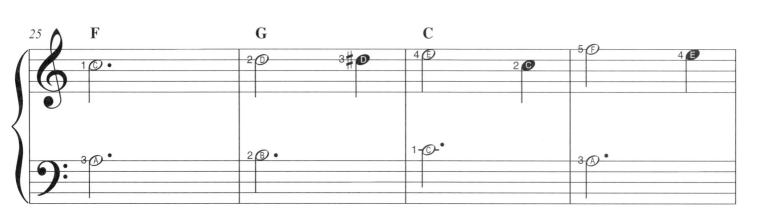

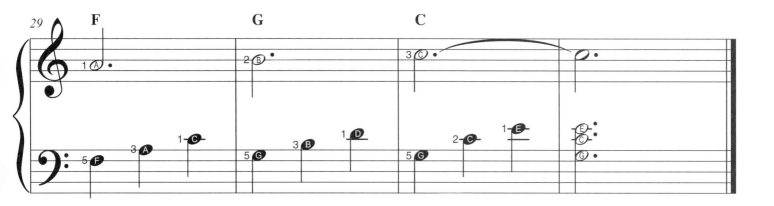

## EIGHTH NOTES

The *eighth note* is another type of note you should learn to play. An eighth note looks a lot like a quarter note, except that it has a flag attached to its stem.

Groups of two or more eighth notes are connected by a bar:

## HOW TO COUNT THEM

You already know that quarter notes get one beat, so the logical question seems to be, "How do I count eighth notes?" To answer this, we'll compare counting beats to tapping your foot in time to music.

When you tap beats in an even and steady manner, your foot makes two motions – up and down. Therefore, each beat has two parts, or halves – an upbeat and a downbeat. The illustration shows this, along with a slightly different way of counting – each downbeat gets a number and each upbeat gets the word "and" (&). Start by slowly tapping your foot and counting aloud. Then try it again, playing the four quarter notes. You'll quickly see how this works.

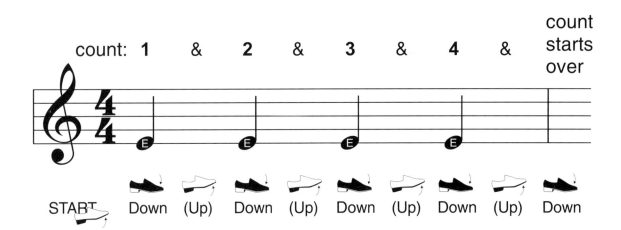

This is the same as the previous example with some eighth notes added. Count and play it a few times.

## JINGLE BELLS

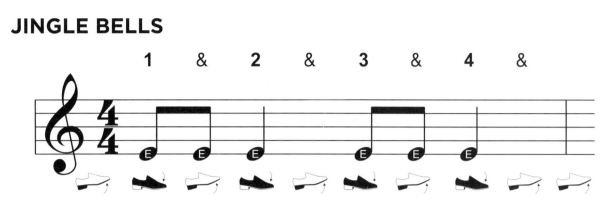

We can now say that an eighth note is one half-beat long. Therefore, two eighth notes are equal to one quarter note.

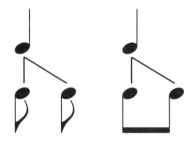

# FRÈRE JACQUES
## (Are You Sleeping?)

Traditional

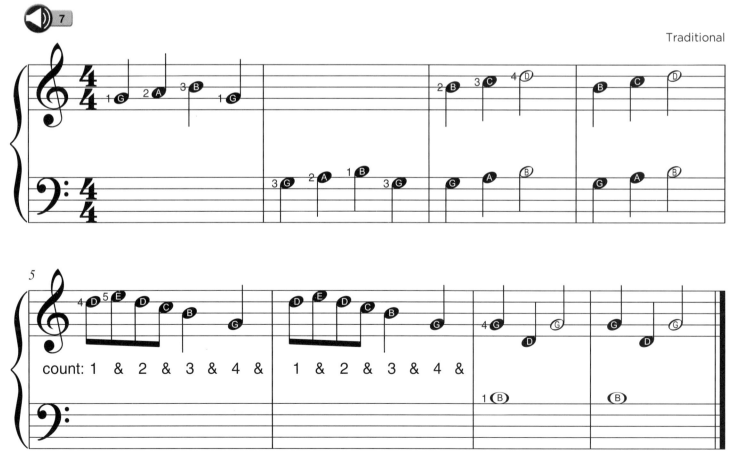

# LAVENDER'S BLUE

English Folksong

**With a lilt**

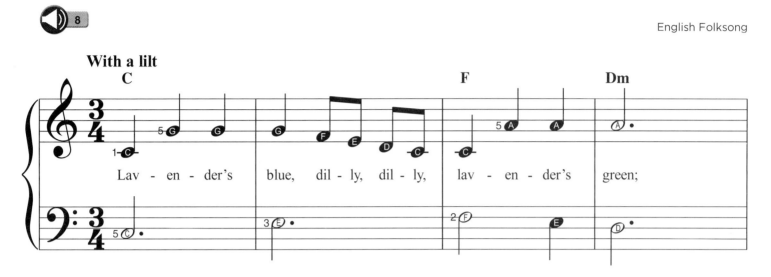

Lav - en - der's blue, dil - ly, dil - ly, lav - en - der's green;

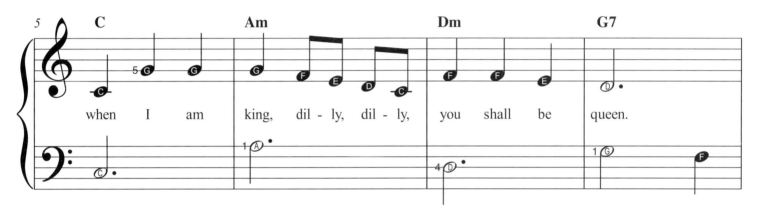

when I am king, dil - ly, dil - ly, you shall be queen.

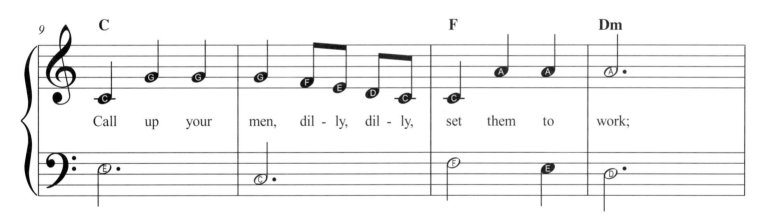

Call up your men, dil - ly, dil - ly, set them to work;

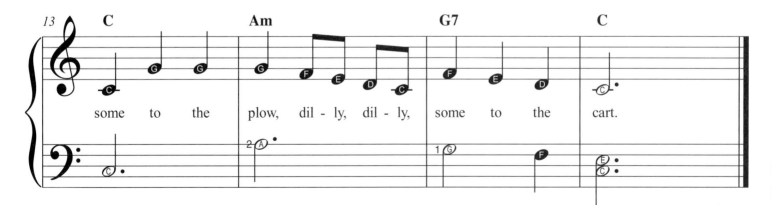

some to the plow, dil - ly, dil - ly, some to the cart.

# Greensleeves

## FLAT ♭

The flat sign (♭) appears before a note to indicate a lowering of the pitch (the sound of the note).

To find B♭, first locate B on the keyboard. B♭ is the very next key to the left. It is a black note. Any flat key is the one immediately to the left, whether black or white.

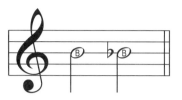

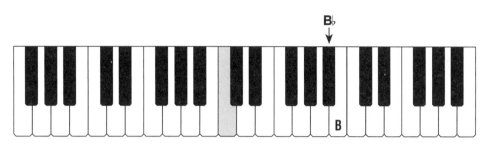

In "Greensleeves," C♯ notes appear in each staff, and the D minor and A minor chords occur for the first time. Locate these before you play the song.

## ARPEGGIO

An *arpeggio* is an exciting, professional sound that occurs when the notes of a chord are played one-at-a-time as your hands move up the keyboard. Be sure to hold down the sustain pedal when you play an arpeggio.

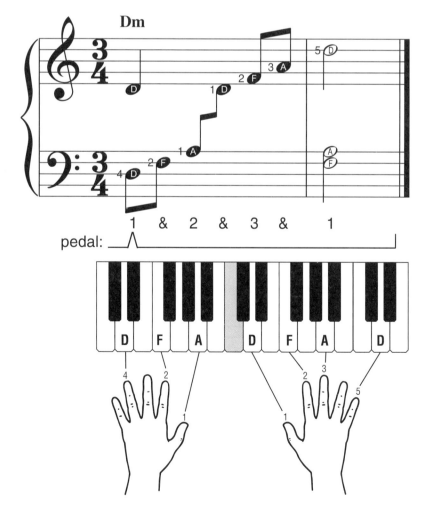

# GREENSLEEVES

16th Century Traditional English

**Flowing**

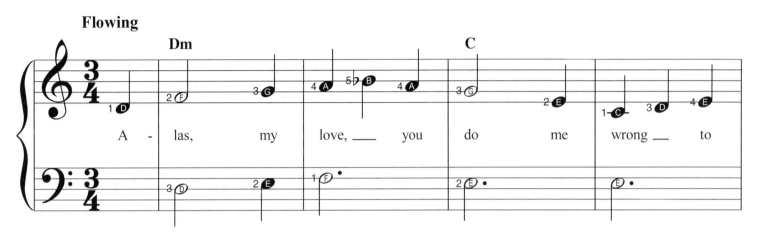

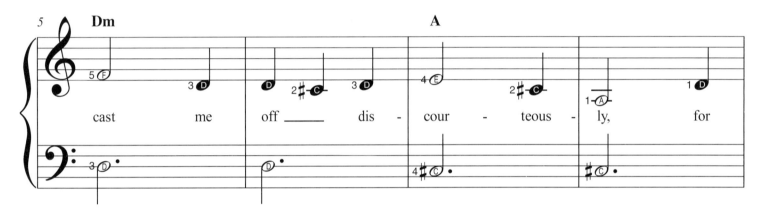

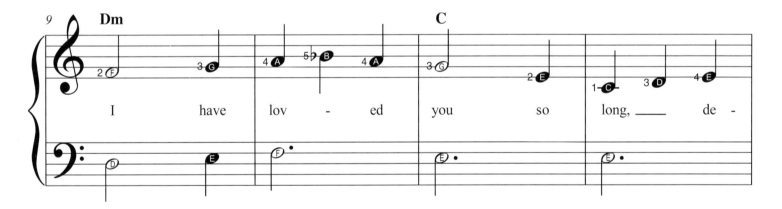

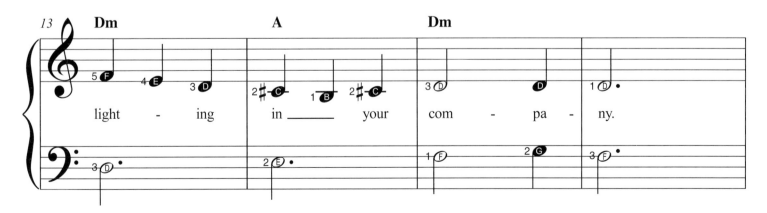

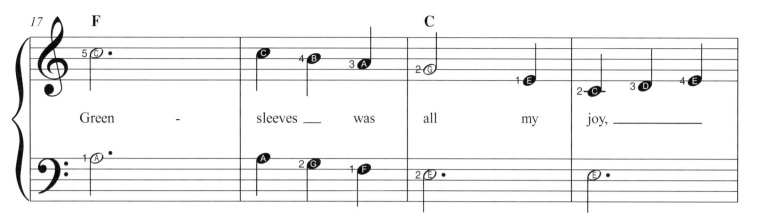

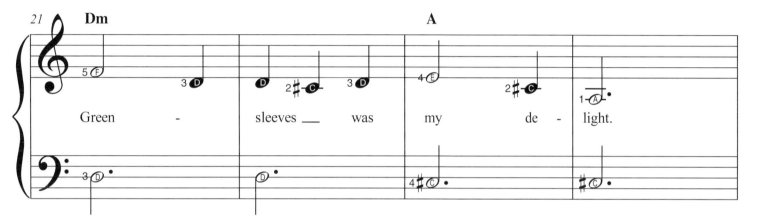

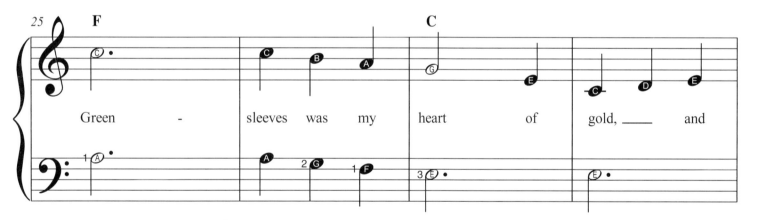

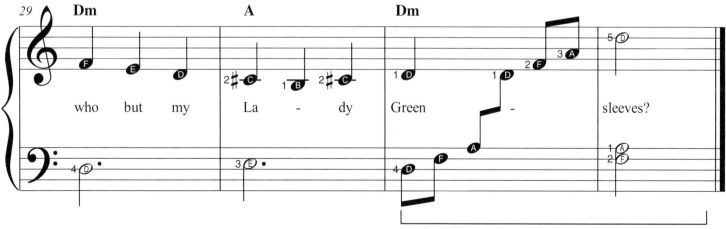

sustain pedal

## RESTS

*Rests* represent silence in music. They tell you when *not* to play. Rests have values just as notes do. Certain rests correspond to certain notes.

| eighth rest | quarter rest | half rest | whole rest |
|:---:|:---:|:---:|:---:|
| ⅞ | ⸓ | ▬ | ▬ |
| ½ beat of silence | 1 beat of silence | 2 beats of silence | 4 beats of silence (or entire measure) |
| eighth note | quarter note | half note | whole note |
| ♪ | ♩ | 𝅗𝅥 | 𝅝 |
| ½ beat | 1 beat | 2 beats | 4 beats |

## NATURAL SIGN ♮

To cancel a sharp or flat, a *natural sign* (♮) is placed in front of a note. In measure 31 of the Rachmaninoff theme that follows, you see an F♯ in the left hand, followed by an F♮. In fact, most of the sharp, flat, and natural signs in the piece appear in the bass staff.

Practice the melody and accompaniment separately before playing them together. Notice that most of the sharp, flat, and natural signs, called accidentals, appear in the bass staff.

## OCTAVE SIGN *8va*

When this sign is placed above a note or group of notes, it indicates that you should play those notes one octave (eight notes) higher than they're written. In other words, move to the right on your keyboard to the next key having the same letter name. This occurs frequently in sheet music notation and makes reading notes outside the staff much easier.

Except for the last three notes, the melody on page 38 is to be played an octave higher than written. The accompaniment, however, does not change.

## LOCO

At the bottom of page 38, you'll see the term *loco*, an Italian word meaning "place." This cancels the *8va* sign and indicates that the melody notes are to be played as written.

# THEME FROM PIANO CONCERTO NO. 2

By Sergei Rachmaninoff
Op. 18

**Moderately**

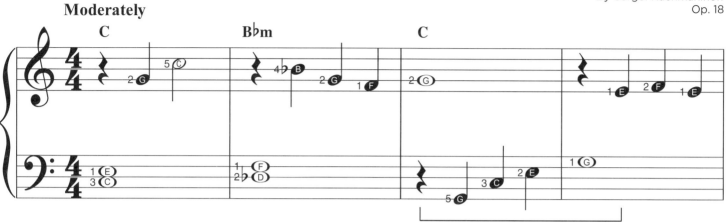

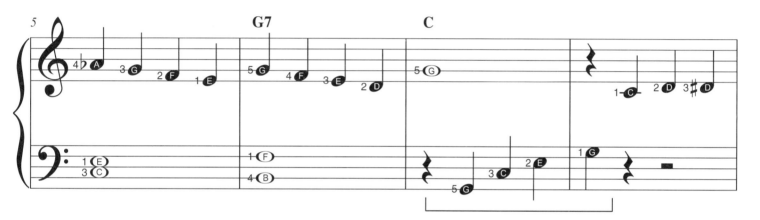

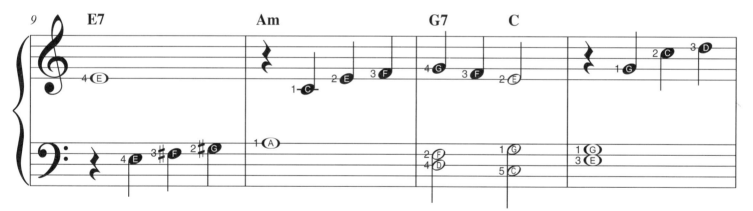

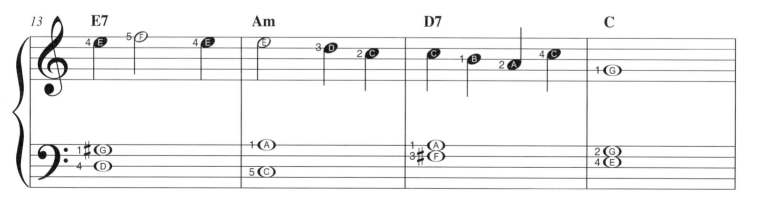

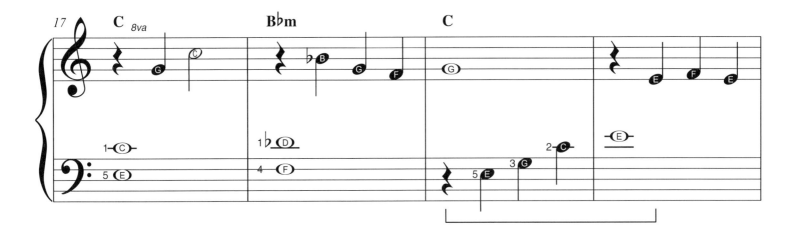

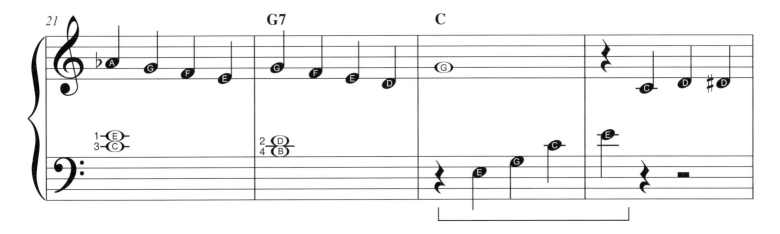

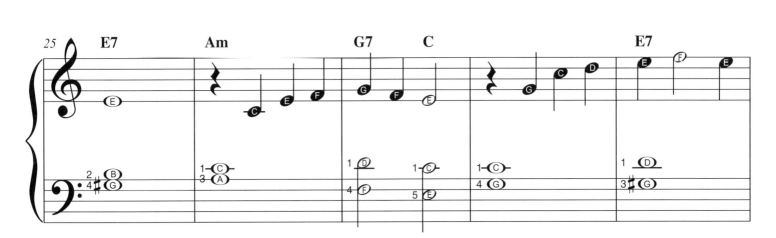

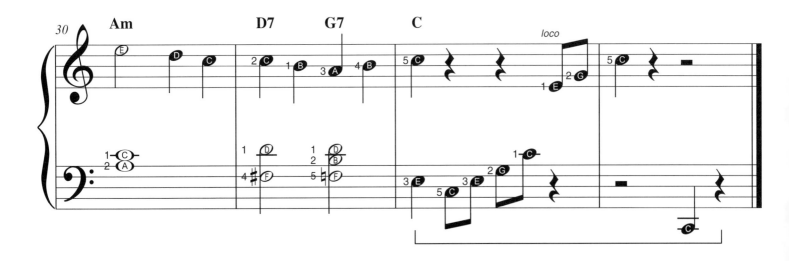

# Review Quiz

Circle the correct answer.

1. What kind of note receives four beats?

   A. half note
   B. quarter note
   C. whole note

2. The two large numbers at the beginning make up the

   A. lines and spaces.
   B. time signature.
   C. fingering.

3. Measures are formed by drawing

   A. bar lines.
   B. clef signs.
   C. chord symbols.

4. How many beats are there in each measure of a song having a 3/4 time signature?

   A. four beats
   B. three beats
   C. seven beats

5. How many beats does a half note receive?

   A. 1/2 beat
   B. one beat
   C. two beats

6. Which of these is an eighth note?

   A. ♪

   B. ♩

   C. 𝅝

7. What is the symbol for a sharp?

   A. 𝄽

   B. $\frac{4}{4}$

   C. ♯

8. What sign means "eight notes higher than written"?

   A. 8*va*

   B. ♮

   C. ▬

9. Which of these is a whole note?

   A. ♩.

   B. 𝅝

   C. ♫

10. Which of these is a quarter rest?

   A. ▬

   B. 𝄾

   C. 𝄽

# CHORD CHART

**CHORDS USED IN PART 1**

(C, F, and G chords are on page 23.)

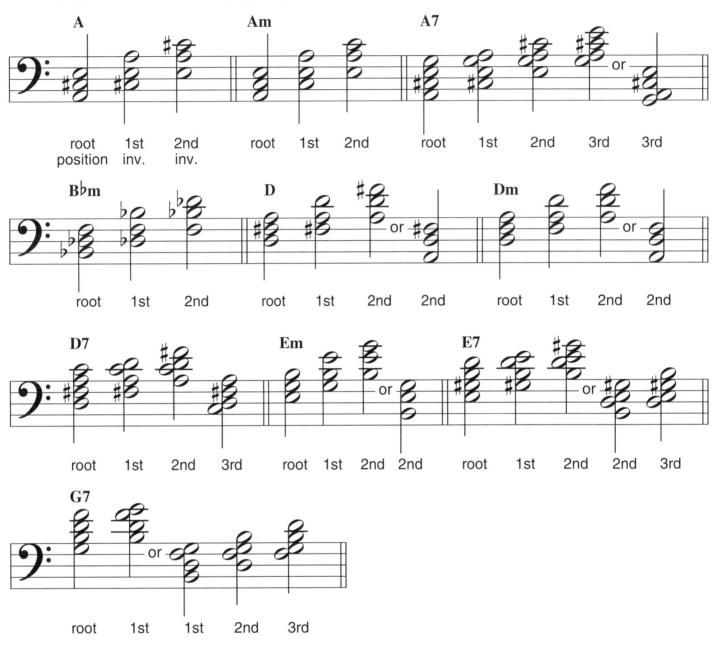

## CHORD SYMBOLS

Chord symbols name the chord and the notes used. Since chord symbols are a form of abbreviation, or shorthand, you should be aware of what the different components mean.

M = major (capital M never appears next to the chord letter; it is understood to be a major chord.)

7 = seventh

m = minor

6 = sixth

9 = ninth

+ = augmented

o = diminished

Sometimes these elements are combined:

m6 = minor sixth

M7 = major seventh

# CONGRATULATIONS!

You've just completed Part 1 of this course and look at what you've learned! In addition, you've been able to entertain yourself and others with some great songs that are enjoyable and easy to play.

Part 2 of *Easy Adult Piano Beginner's Course* will prepare you for the Easy Pro arrangements. These are a definite step up from Easy Beginner, being more pianistic and professional-sounding, yet still easy to play.

Before you begin Part 2, you may want to look over the following material.

# REVIEW OF PART 1

## STAFF AND NOTES

All piano music is written on a *grand staff*, which consists of a *treble staff* and a *bass staff*, connected by a bracket.

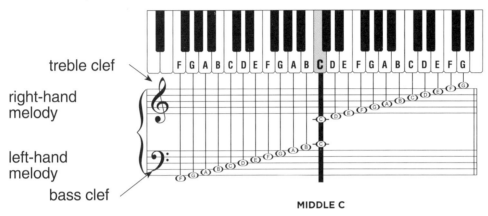

MIDDLE C

## MEASURES AND BAR LINES

The staff is divided into sections by using vertical lines called *bar lines*. The sections between the bar lines are called *measures*.

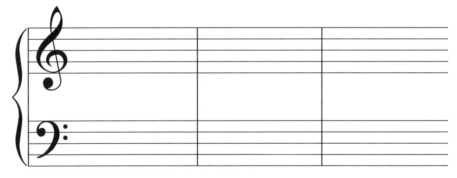

## TIME VALUES

In music, time is measured in *beats*. The illustration shows the types of notes you'll play and how many beats each type gets.

Rests are shown in the lower part of the illustration, along with the number of beats each type gets. A *rest* indicates a period of silence, when you don't play; they still must be counted, however.

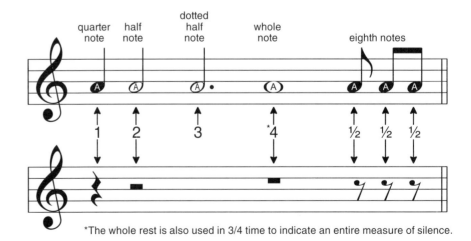

*The whole rest is also used in 3/4 time to indicate an entire measure of silence.

## TIME SIGNATURE

The two numbers at the beginning of a song are known as the *time signature*. The top number indicates the number of beats in each measure. The bottom number 4 tells you each quarter note ( ♩ ) receives one beat.

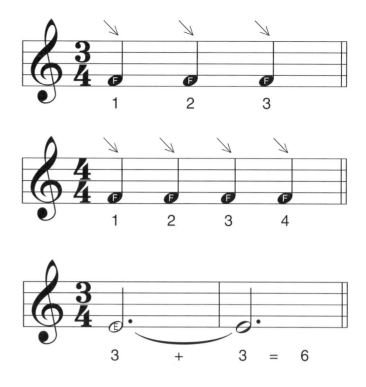

## TIES

A *tie* connects notes on the same line or in the same space. It tells you the first note is struck and then held for the total time value of the tied notes.

## PLAYING THE BLACK KEYS

Sharps and flats tell you when to play the black keys. A *sharp* (♯) tells you to play the very next key to the right and a *flat* (♭) tells you to play the very next key to the left. *Natural signs* (♮) are used to cancel sharps and flats.

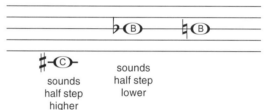

## FINGERING

Small numbers appear near some of the notes; these are *finger numbers* and they'll help you play more smoothly. Fingers are numbered as shown. Play the piano keys with the fingers that correspond to the numbers near the notes.

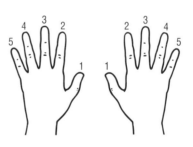

## OCTAVE SIGN

This sign tells you to play an *octave higher*. In other words, move to the right on your keyboard to the next key having the same letter name.

## PICK-UP NOTES

*Pick-up notes* are any notes played before the first complete measure of a song is played. The example below has a 3/4 time signature, but the first measure has only two beats; the third beat appears at the end of the song.

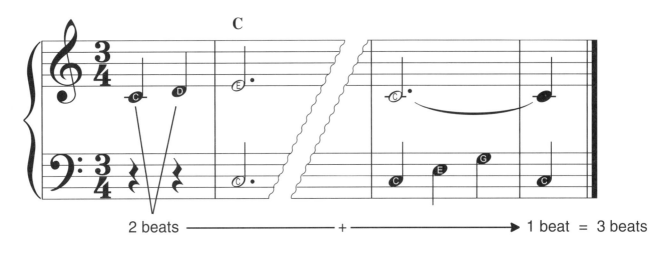

## THE SUSTAIN PEDAL

Regardless of how many pedals your piano has, the one pedal present on all pianos is called the *sustain pedal*.

When you play a key and at the same time press down this pedal, the musical tone continues to sustain, or linger, long after your fingers have left the keys. This can help you create a big, full sound if you use the pedal properly.

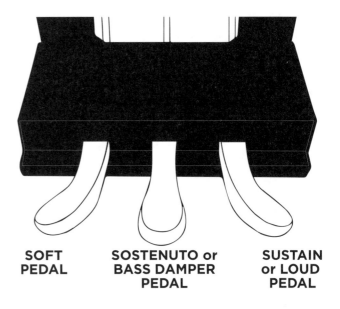

**SOFT PEDAL**   **SOSTENUTO or BASS DAMPER PEDAL**   **SUSTAIN or LOUD PEDAL**

# NAME THE KEYS

Name the circled keys. Check your answers when you're finished.

Do this until you can name the keys correctly.

**1.**

**2.**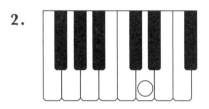

**3.**

**4.**

**5.**

**6.**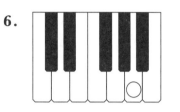

**7.**

**8.**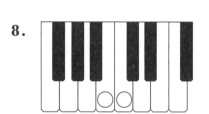

**9.**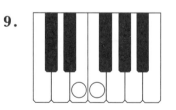

Write the names of the lines and spaces in the illustrations below.

Helpful hint: Use middle C as a reference point. Notice, as notes skip from line to line, or space to space, you skip a letter.

**Lines**

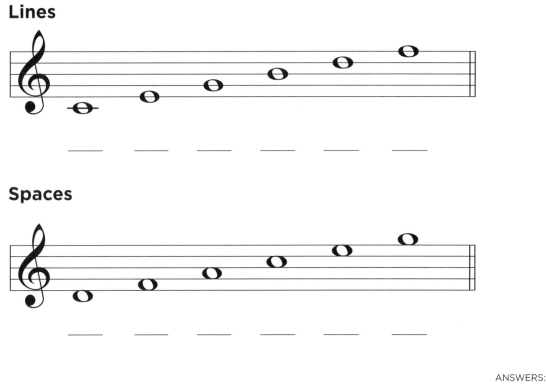

**Spaces**

As practice in reading notes, write the names of the notes in the exercise below.

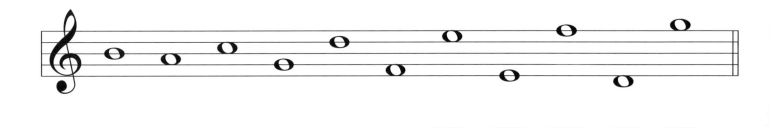

46

## LEGER LINES
## Also "Ledger Lines"

You've already seen notes written on small lines placed above or below the staff. These are called *leger lines* (or *ledger lines*) and are an extension of the staff. Though leger lines are not as long as the regular lines of the staff, they do represent specific keys on the keyboard. Notes written on leger lines are shown.

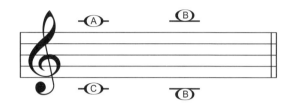

Write in the names of the notes appearing on leger lines in the next illustration.

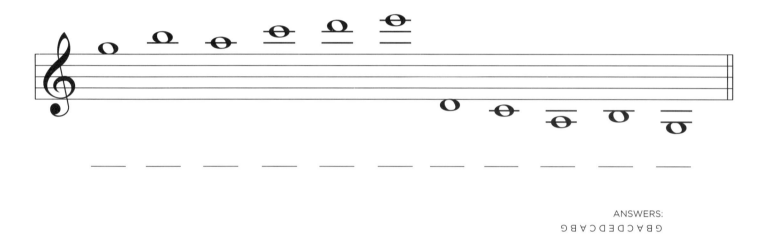

In the examples below, draw a line from the notes to the correct key. Middle C is indicated in gray to help you.

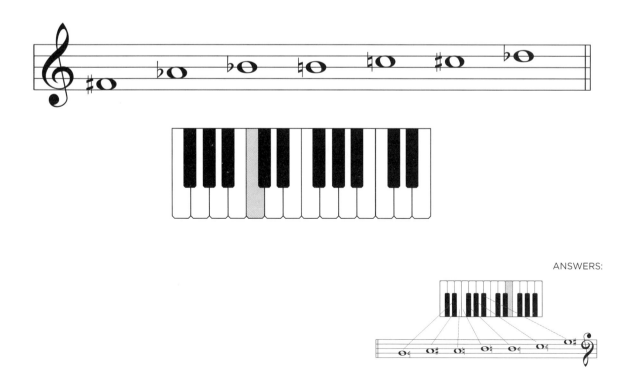

ANSWERS:

# Notes:

# Du, Du Liegst Mir Im Herzen

## SCALES

A *scale* is a series of eight notes that begins on a given line or space and ends on the next line or space with the same letter name. Each of the notes is a specific distance from the others in the series; this distance is measured in whole steps and half steps. Although there are several kinds of scales, the most common is the major scale. The starting note of the scale determines the letter-name of the scale. (The C scale starts on C, the F scale starts on F, etc.) The C, F, and G major scales are shown; notice that the pattern of whole steps (W) and half steps (H) is the same in each case.

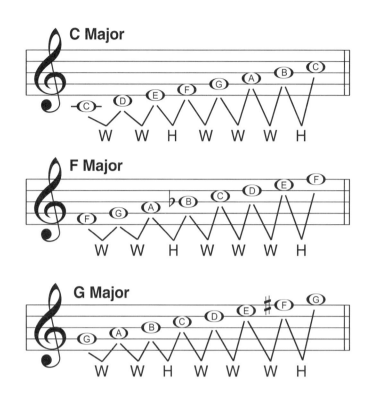

## KEY SIGNATURES

In many songs, you'll see one or more sharps or flats printed at the beginning of the music, after the clef sign. This is called the *key signature*.

The word *key* means the key-note, or principal note, around which the other tones of a particular song are organized. *Key* also refers to the scale upon which the song is based. The first note of the scale is the same as the key-note of the song.

Any note whose sharp or flat appears in the key signature is to be played sharp or flat throughout the entire song. A song having no sharps or flats in its key signature is based on the C major scale and is said to be "written in the key of C major."

## DOUBLE NOTES

"Du, du liegst mir im Herzen" is the first song in which you'll play double notes with your right hand; along with the melody note, you'll also play a harmony note. Double notes occur starting at measures 17 and 25. Fingering is suggested to help you; be sure to practice these passages separately before you play the entire arrangement.

# DU, DU LIEGST MIR IM HERZEN

## (You, You Are in My Heart)

**Key:** G major

German Folksong

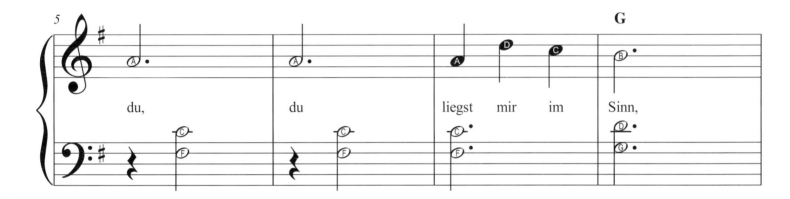

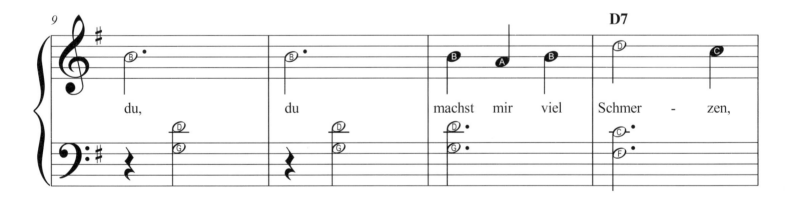

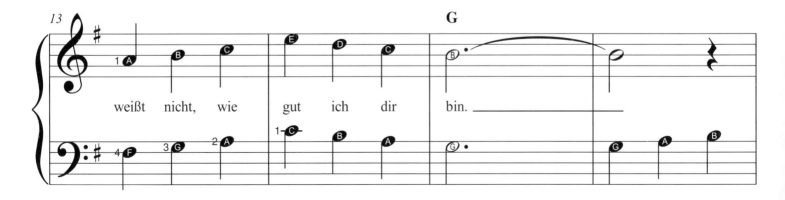

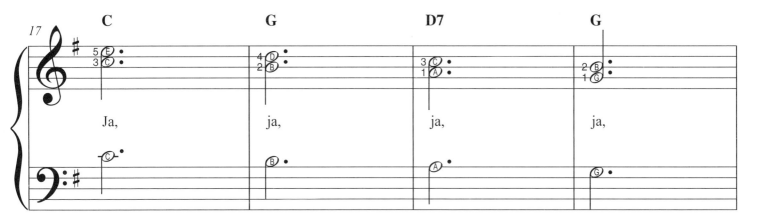

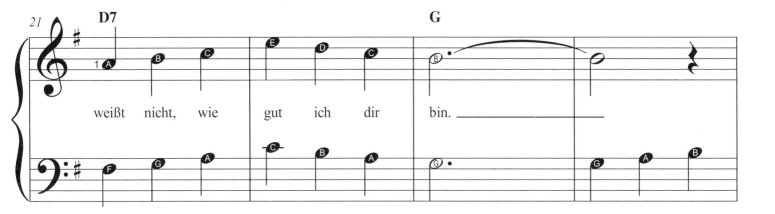

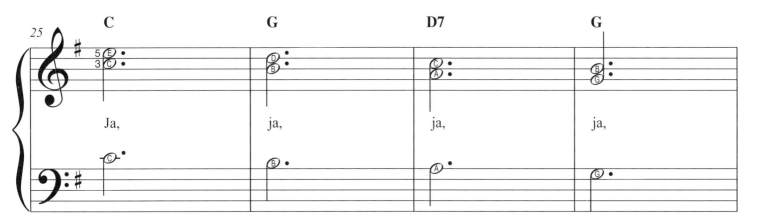

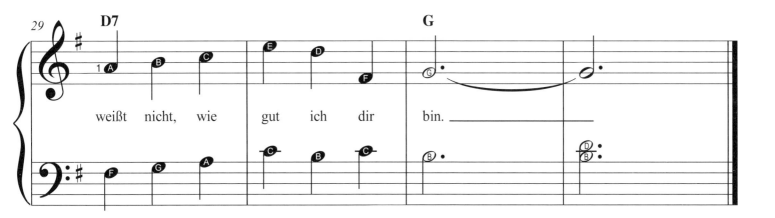

## D.S. AL CODA

You'll notice some new symbols in this song because it has a *coda*. Coda is the Italian word for "tail," so we use it to refer to a short section of music used to end a song.

At measure 16, you'll see the phrase *D.S. al Coda*, which is shorthand for *dal segno al coda*. Segno is the Italian word for "sign," so D.S. al Coda tells you to go back to this sign 𝄋 and replay the measures until you reach this instruction: To Coda ⊕. Then skip to the coda. The illustration below shows you how it works. If you need further clarification, refer to the demo on Track 12.

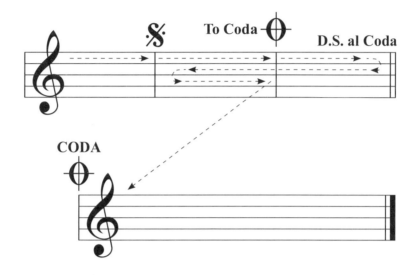

## FERMATA 𝄐

The *fermata sign* indicates a pause, or a hold. Fermata signs appear at the very end of "Vienna Life" and tell you to hold the notes longer than the indicated value. Again, refer to the demo track.

# VIENNA LIFE

**Key: C major**

By Johann Strauss, Jr.
Op. 354

Moderate Waltz tempo

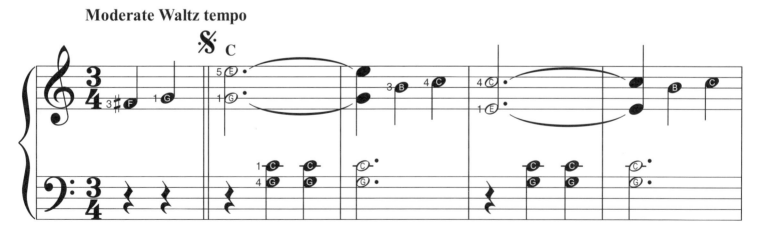

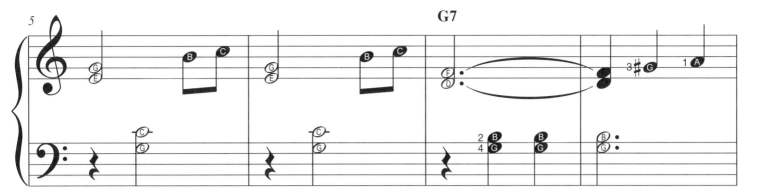

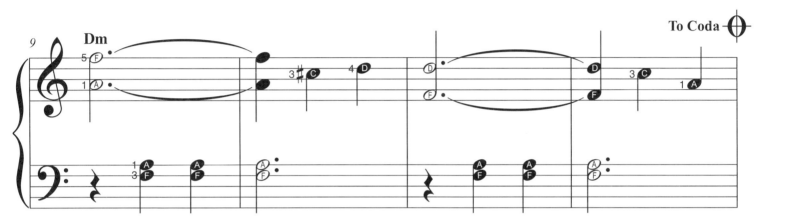

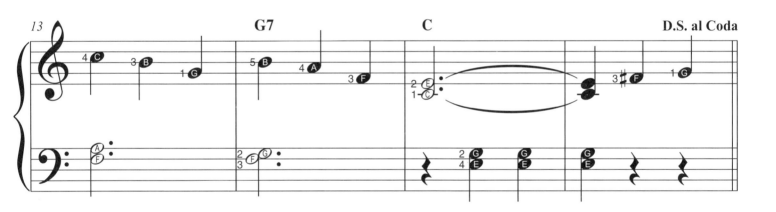

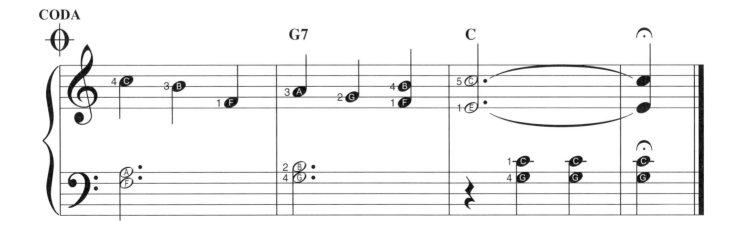

So far, you've played songs with notes-that-name-themselves. "Bill Bailey, Won't You Please Come Home" is the first song you'll play that has no letters in the melody. This helps prepare you for the Easy Pro arrangements found in the Easy Favorites section, which also have no letters in the melody. All songs from now on have no letters in the treble staff.

This should be easy for you since you've played so many songs with letters in the notes; you've already learned most of them by association. In addition, many people can already read notes on the treble staff because of playing experience on other instruments (flute, violin, etc.). The example here reminds you that the letter-names of the spaces spell the word FACE and the letter-names of the lines, E-G-B-D-F, can be remembered with Every Good Boy Does Fine.

You also have the A-B-C key stickers to help you. Just match the notes to those shown on the keys. Playing through a melody a couple of times with your right hand will help you become more familiar with the names of the notes. Then add the left-hand accompaniment.

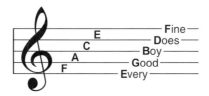

## INTRODUCTIONS

*Introductions* are used in music to "set up" or "get into" the mood of a song. Sometimes introductions, usually four to eight measures long, use parts of the melody or an important rhythm that appears in the song itself. The introduction to "Bill Bailey, Won't You Please Come Home" is based on the last four measures of the song.

# BILL BAILEY, WON'T YOU PLEASE COME HOME

**Key: F major**

Words and Music by
Hughie Cannon

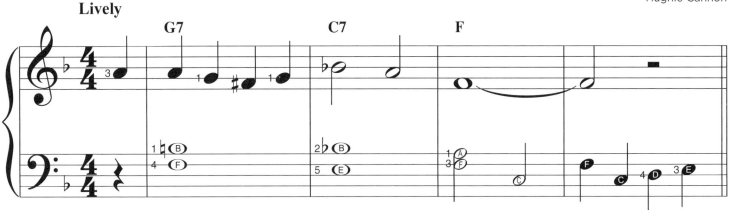

Won't you come home, Bill Bai-ley, won't you come home?

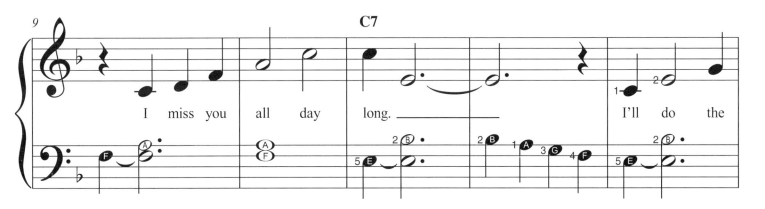

I miss you all day long. _____ I'll do the

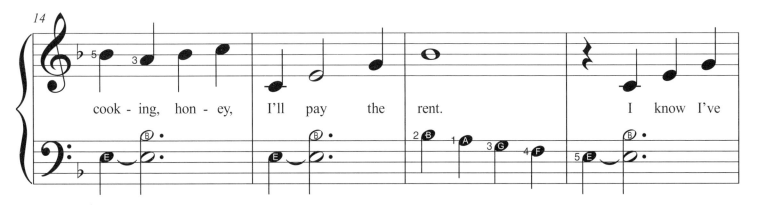

cook-ing, hon-ey, I'll pay the rent. I know I've

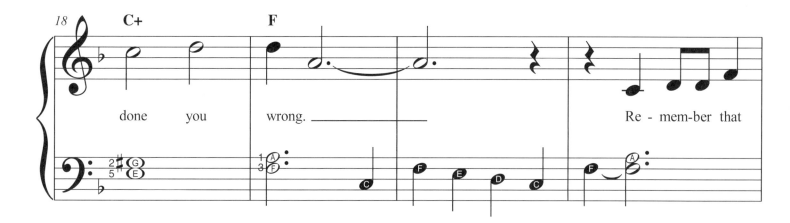

done you wrong. _____ Re - mem-ber that

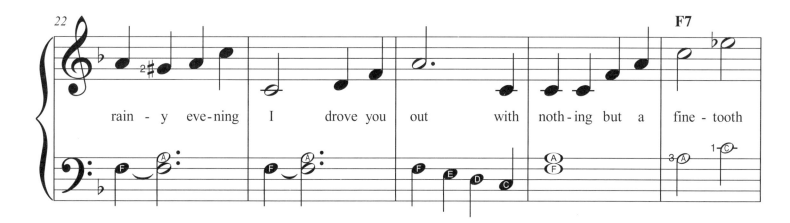

rain - y eve-ning I drove you out with noth-ing but a fine - tooth

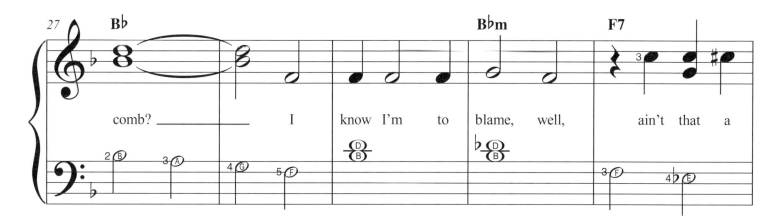

comb? _____ I know I'm to blame, well, ain't that a

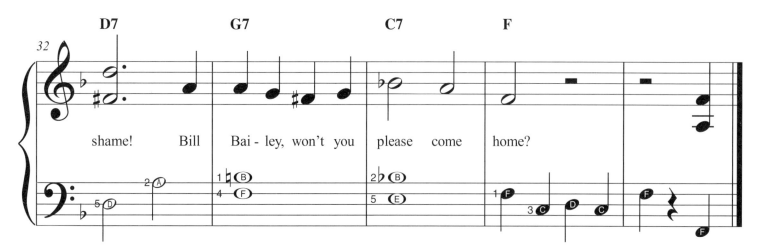

shame! Bill Bai - ley, won't you please come home?

# DANUBE WAVES

## REPEAT SIGNS

Quite often, a song has more than one set of lyrics, or a part of a song needs to be played a second time. Instead of printing that section again, *repeat signs* are used.

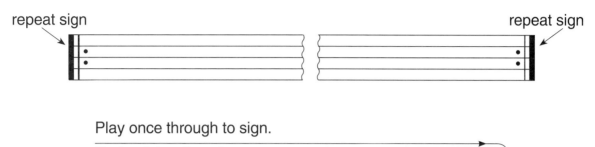

## DOUBLE ENDINGS

Some songs have more than one ending. In these cases, a *double ending* is used.

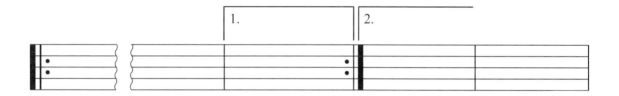

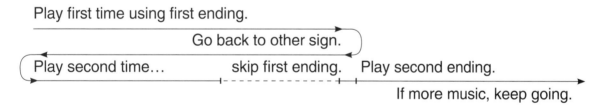

Other things to notice about this arrangement:

- "Danube Waves" is written in the key of A minor. (Clue: The last chord symbol in a song often indicates the key.) A minor has the same key signature as C major – no sharps or flats. This makes them *relative keys*.

- The left-hand part consists of pyramid chords, chords whose notes are played one-at-a-time and held. Practice the accompaniment alone before you play hands together.

- The end of "Danube Waves" features a type of arpeggio you've played before. Practice this part separately, using the sustain pedal.

# DANUBE WAVES

**Key: A minor**

By Iosif Ivanovici

**Moderate Waltz tempo**

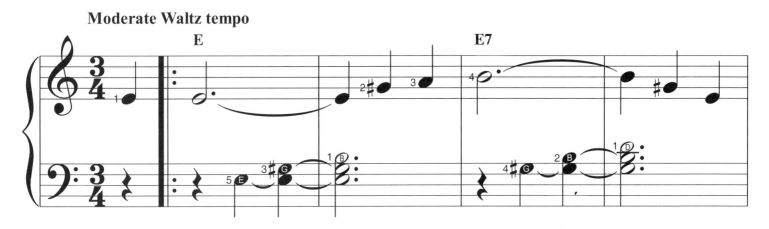

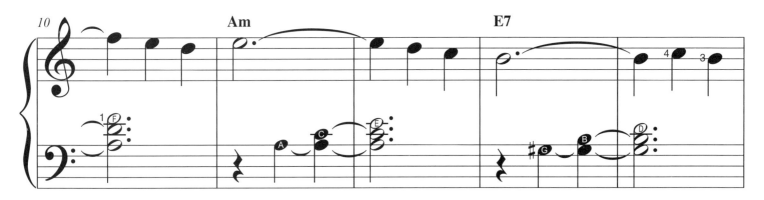

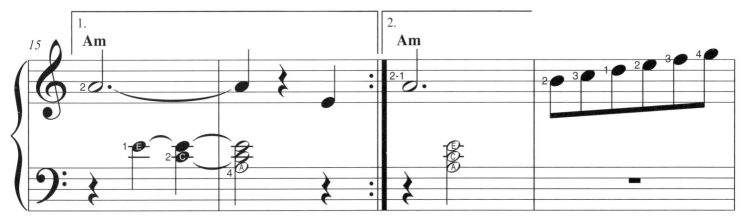

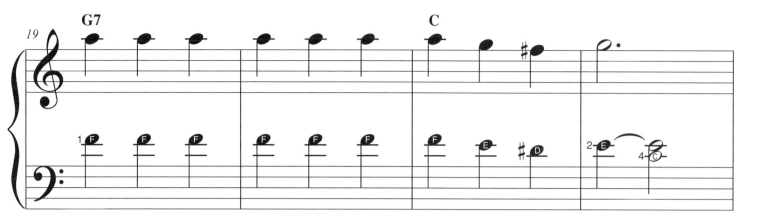

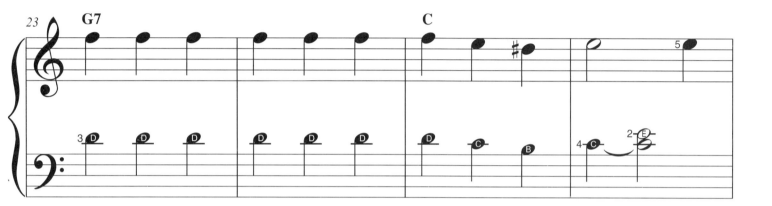

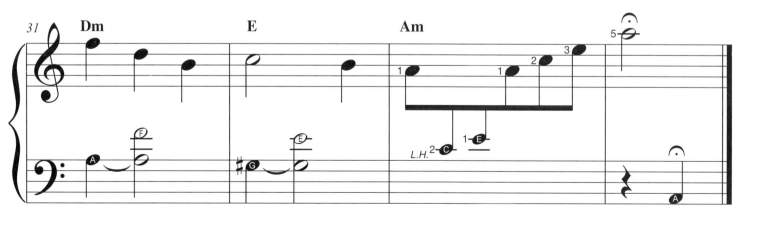

# KUMBAYA

## DOTTED-QUARTER NOTES

**Rule: A dot placed after a note increases the time value of the note by one-half.**

You saw this applied to the dotted-half note (2 beats + 1 beat) back in Part 1; here's how it applies in the case of dotted-quarter notes.

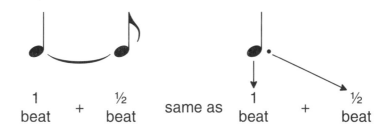

Most often, a dotted-quarter note is followed by an eighth note for a total time value of two beats (1-1/2 + 1/2 = 2). This is the way the dotted-quarter notes appear in "Kumbaya." The next example shows how counting and foot-taps apply. Play it a few times.

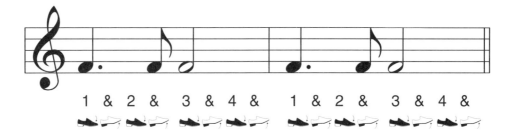

Musicians often refer to this as the *soft-rock pattern*, especially when it is played by an instrument such as the bass guitar.

Try this excerpt from a well-known Christmas carol.

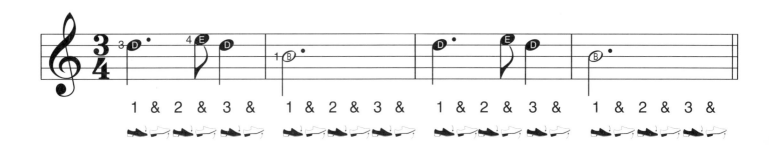

60

# KUMBAYA

**Key: C major**

Congo Folksong

**Moderately**

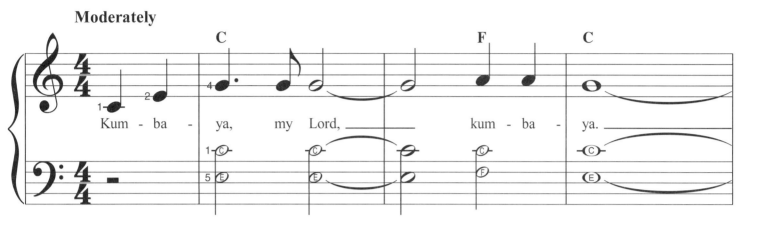

Kum - ba - ya, my Lord, _____ kum - ba - ya. _____

_____ Kum - ba - ya, my Lord, _____ kum - ba - ya.

_____ Kum - ba - ya, my Lord, _____ kum - ba - ya. _____

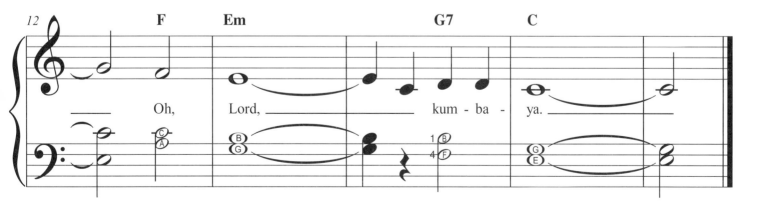

_____ Oh, Lord, _____ kum - ba - ya.

# REVIEW QUIZ

## A. NAME THE NOTES

By naming the notes below, you can decode the message.

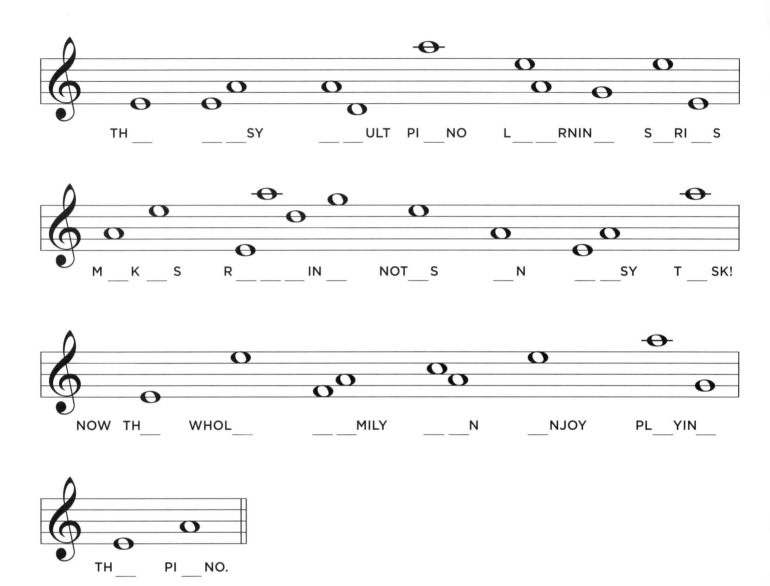

TH__  __ __SY  __ __ULT  PI__NO  L__RNIN__  S__RI__S

M__K__S  R__ __ __IN__  NOT__S  __N  __ __SY  T__SK!

NOW  TH__  WHOL__  __ __MILY  __ __N  __NJOY  PL__YIN__

TH__  PI__NO.

# B. MATCHING

Match the numbers in the left column to the correct answers on the right.

1. Pick-up notes

2.

3. Octave

4.

5. Measure

6. (repeat signs image)

7. Key signature

8. No sharps or flats

9. **CODA** (coda symbol)

10. F major

11. Introduction

12. Relative

13.

14. Scale

15. G major

(  ) Major and minor keys having the same key signature

(  ) Eight notes apart

(  ) Notes played before the first chord is played

(  ) Pause or hold

(  ) Sometimes called the "soft-rock" rhythm

(  ) Space between two bar lines

(  ) Establishes the mood of a song

(  ) One sharp in a key signature

(  ) Key of C major

(  ) Orderly series of notes based on a whole-step/half-step pattern

(  ) Worth 1-1/2 beats

(  ) Indicates the scale on which the song is based

(  ) One flat in a key signature

(  ) Repeat signs

(  ) Part of a song used as the ending

## NATURAL ACCENTS

Although the beats occurring in any measure are equal in time value, some of them are played with an accent that makes them stronger than the others. This helps add variety and a rhythmic feel to music. Consider the OOM-pah-pah of the waltz rhythm; the first beat is always played with more emphasis than the other two. This makes the first beat in each measure of 3/4 time a primary beat; the other two beats are called secondary beats. In 4/4 time, the first and third beats in each measure are considered primary; the second and fourth beats, then, are secondary.

Accent marks (>) help indicate primary beats in the example.

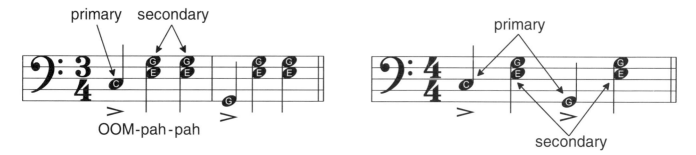

It is the placement of accents that helps music flow rhythmically. It is the placement of accents that also introduces the next subject, syncopation.

## SYNCOPATION

*Syncopation* occurs when accents are placed anywhere but on primary beats. The examples below show how accented secondary beats give a Ragtime feeling to songs from the turn of the 20th century. Play each melody and strike the keys represented by notes marked with accents a bit hard.

# HELLO! MY BABY

# GIVE MY REGARDS TO BROADWAY

Syncopation also occurs when accents fall between the beats in a measure. This is what gives jazz tunes and Latin-American rhythms their distinctive flavors. The first part shows the accents on the primary first and third beats; the second part shows the accents on the first beat and the upbeat ("and") between the second and third beats. The two E notes being tied emphasizes the syncopated feeling when you play. Try it.

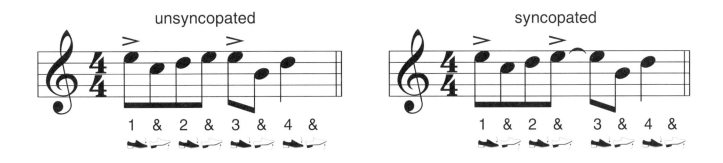

In the second part of the example, you're anticipating the third beat by playing its accent before you actually get to it. You can explore this further by playing the next two examples – the first two measures of "The Entertainer," shown without syncopation, and with.

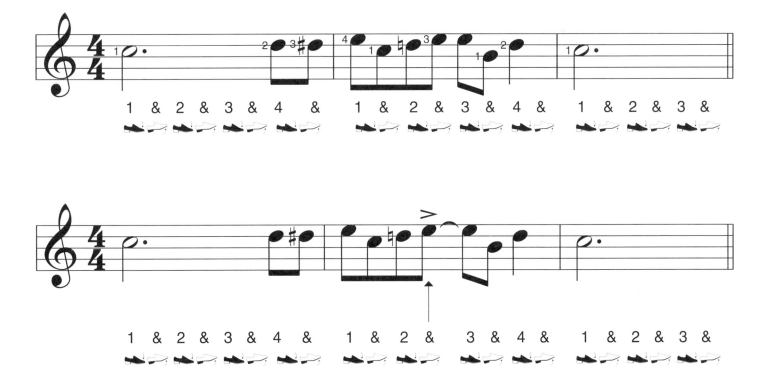

The arrow in the second example is used throughout the arrangement of "The Entertainer" to guide you through the places where syncopation occurs. Take your time and play the melody of the song alone at first, then add the left-hand part. Do the same for "Frankie and Johnny."

# THE ENTERTAINER

**Key: C major**

By Scott Joplin

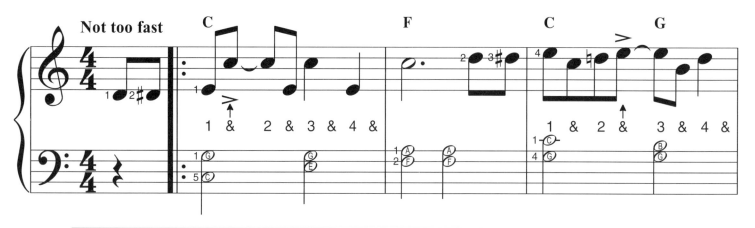

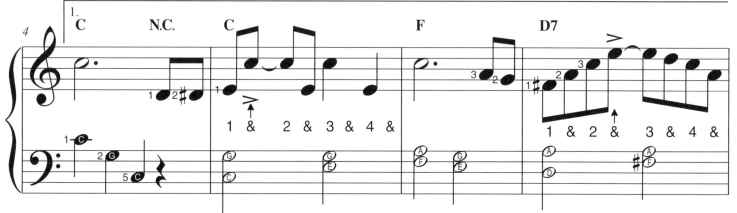

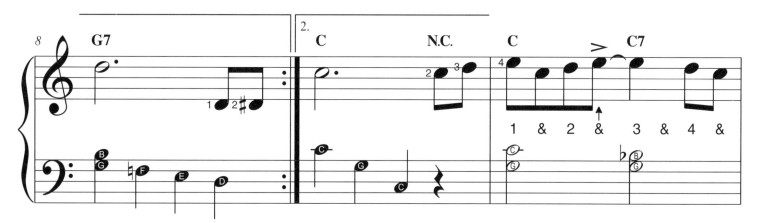

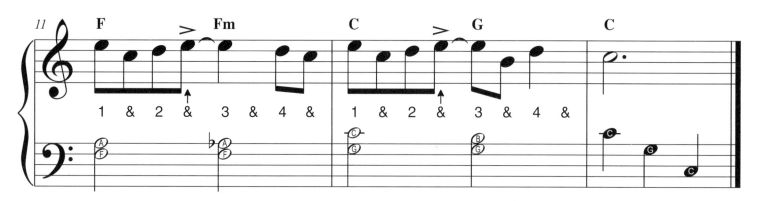

# FRANKIE AND JOHNNY

**Key: C major**

Anonymous Blues Ballad

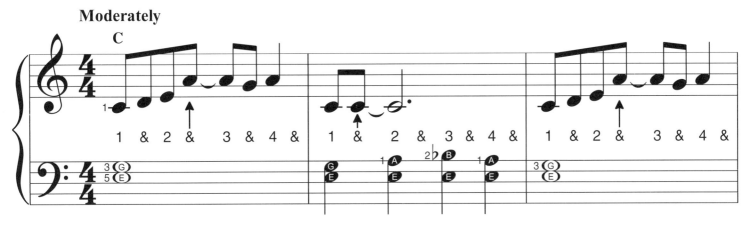

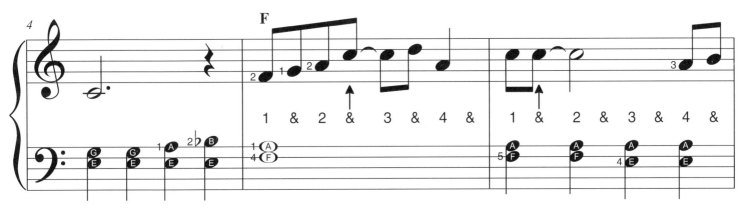

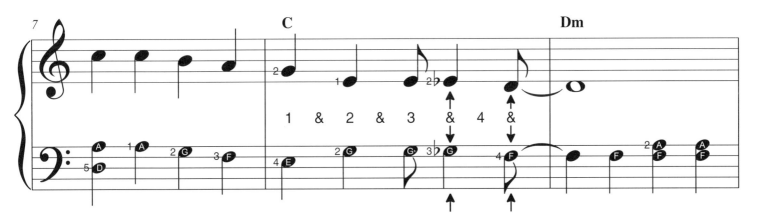

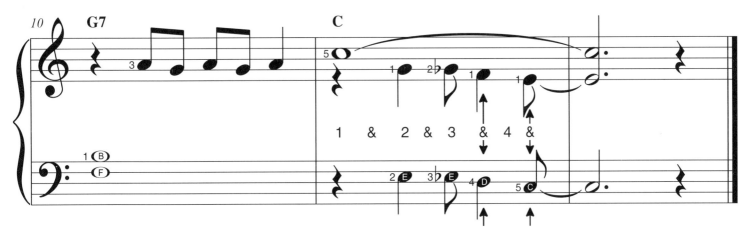

This song gives you additional practice in playing syncopation. As before, arrows are used throughout to guide you. You may want to write in the counting as shown in the first two measures.

Here, the left-hand part is more rhythmic than most of the songs you've played up to now; it will be helpful if you practice it separately at first. Measures 9–15 feature an accompaniment style called *walking bass*. These notes must be played on the beat, especially considering the syncopation that occurs in the melody of the same measures.

# HE'S GOT THE WHOLE WORLD IN HIS HANDS

**Key: C major**

Traditional Spiritual

**Moderately**

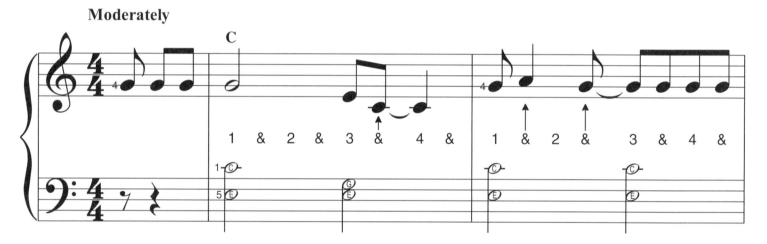

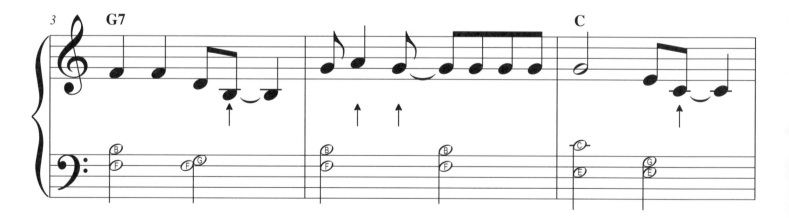

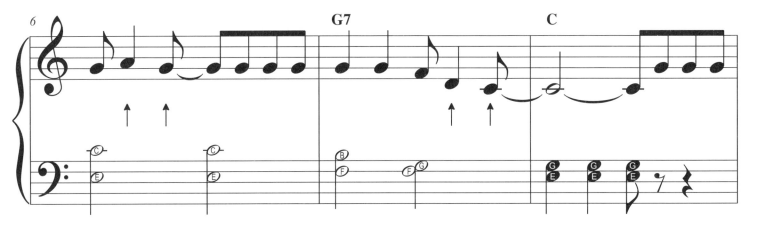

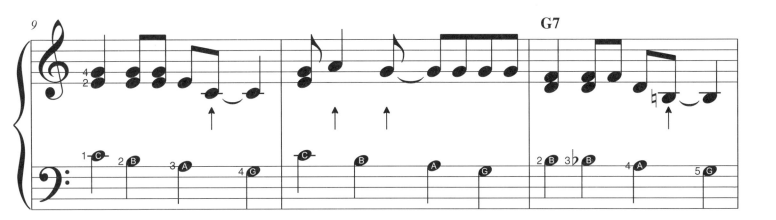

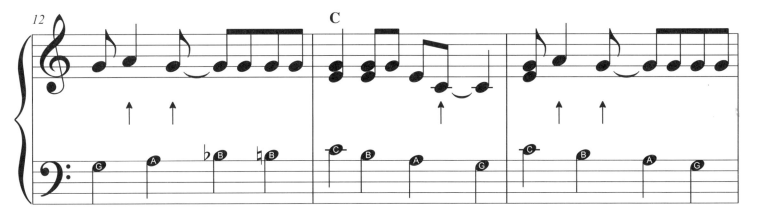

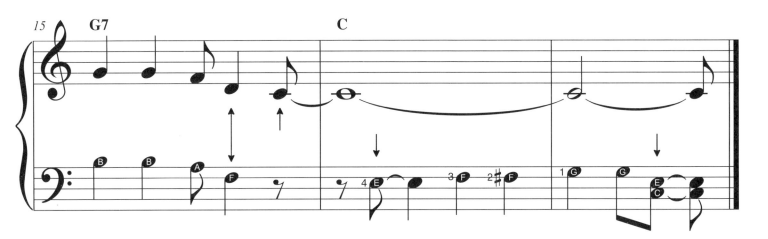

# MICHAEL, ROW THE BOAT ASHORE

## NEW ACCOMPANIMENT STYLE

In the last few years, the piano has been enjoying renewed interest from musicians and listeners alike. In the popular music field especially, the piano, whether acoustic or electronic, has made its presence known on an ever-increasing number of recordings.

The arrangement of "Michael, Row the Boat Ashore" on page 71 features an accompaniment style frequently heard in pop-rock music. Since this involves playing left-hand notes as far apart as an octave, you'll find it helpful to play the examples shown here. They're based on the first line of the arrangement. The first example is in half notes, played at the same time, to help you get used to the wider hand positions. After you've played it a few times, try to do it without looking at your keyboard.

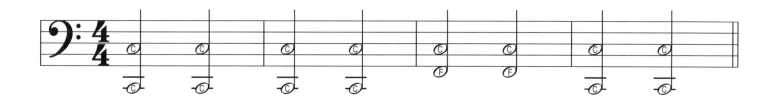

The second example is written in quarter notes, played as they are in the song itself. These should be played in a smooth, legato style.

The left-hand style is also used in a rather unusual arrangement of "When the Saints Go Marching In," and can be found on page 129.

# MICHAEL, ROW THE BOAT ASHORE

**Key: C major**

Traditional Folksong

## MORE ON INTRODUCTIONS

As you learned in "Bill Bailey, Won't You Please Come Home," an *introduction* prepares the listener for the song itself by establishing the tempo and general mood. Most introductions of pop or standard songs are generally four to eight measures long and are usually taken from the song itself.

Many classical composers, on the other hand, created introductions that were, in themselves, mini-compositions of various lengths – some had moods and themes totally different from any part of the main body of the composition.

Johann Strauss II, a famous composer of Viennese waltzes, wrote "Tales from the Vienna Woods." The introduction of this song is 14 measures long and establishes the tempo and general mood of the piece. Its melodic content, however, is not repeated anywhere within the composition.

## MODULATION

*Modulation* is the process of changing from one key (signature) to another in a smooth, logical manner. Generally, it is done to give new life to a song – or a fresh sound – thereby making the arrangement more interesting. This is especially true if the same segment (or the entire song) is to be repeated.

A modulation is also used frequently when playing a medley. It offers a smooth transition, or segue, from one song to another.

Many classical compositions contain different melodic themes located in different segments, or movements. "Tales from the Vienna Woods" contains four distinct sections (excluding the "intro"). The first, in the key of D major, starts at measure 15, the second (also in D major) at measure 43, which acts as a "bridge" into the last two segments starting at measures 58 and 75.

The composition sounds as though it could end in measure 54. However, the composer may have had a fresh idea for a new melody that would better conclude the piece. Measures 55-57 contain a *chord progression* (a sequence of chords) that segues into the third segment in the key of G major.

# TALES FROM THE VIENNA WOODS

**Key: D major**

By Johann Strauss, Jr.
Op. 325

**Moderate Waltz tempo**

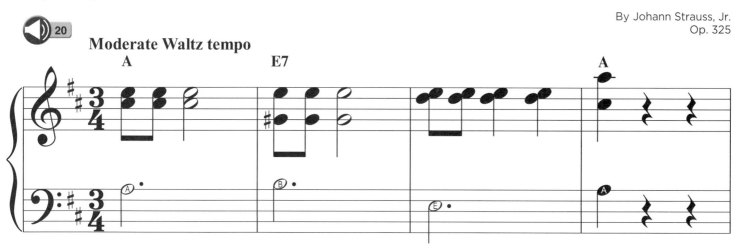

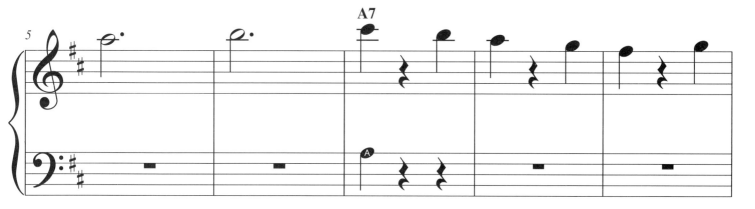

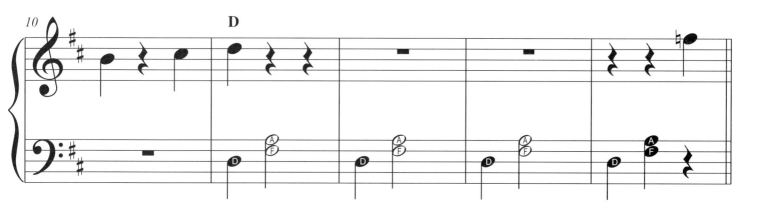

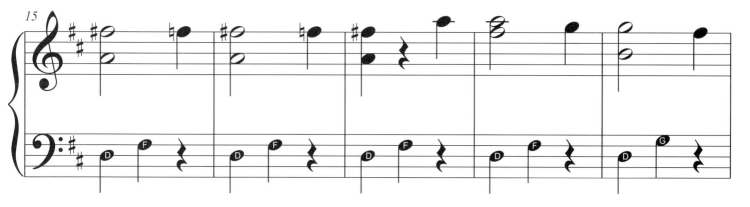

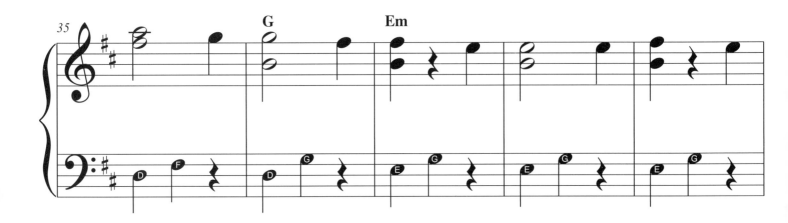

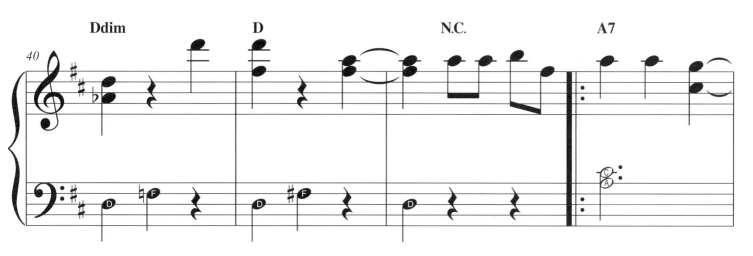

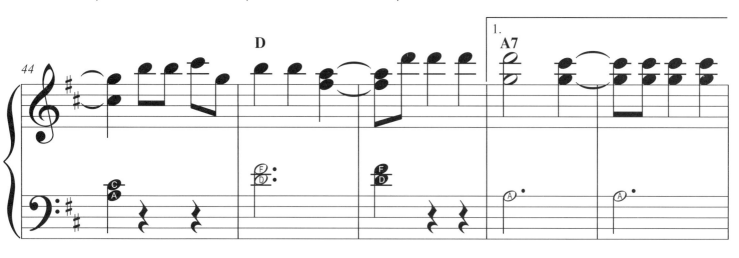

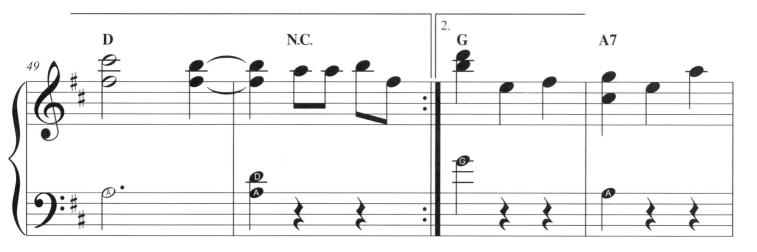

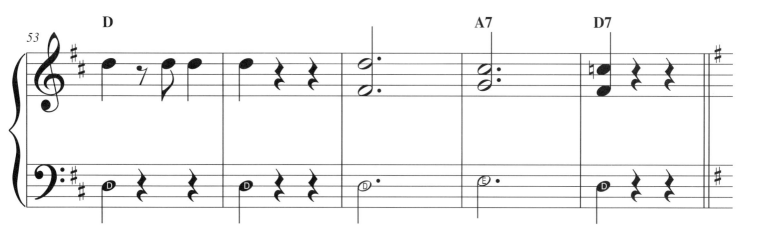

**Key: G major**

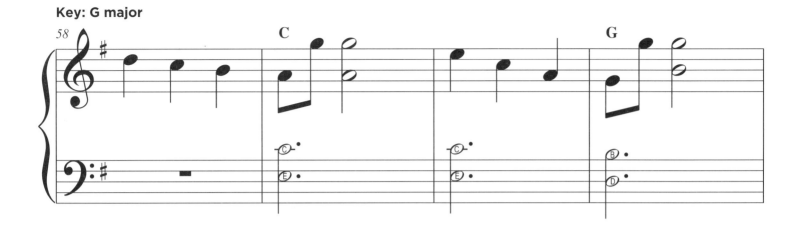

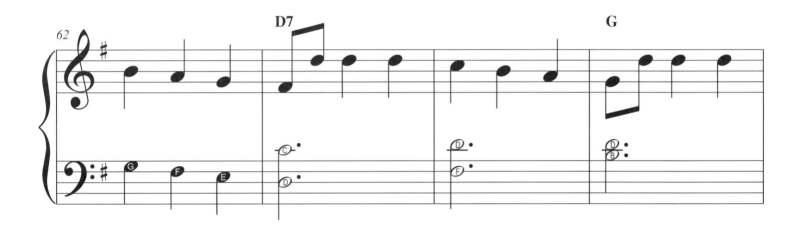

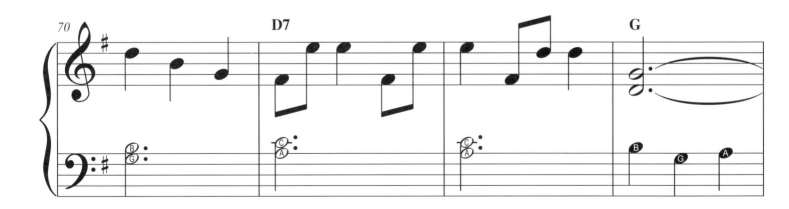

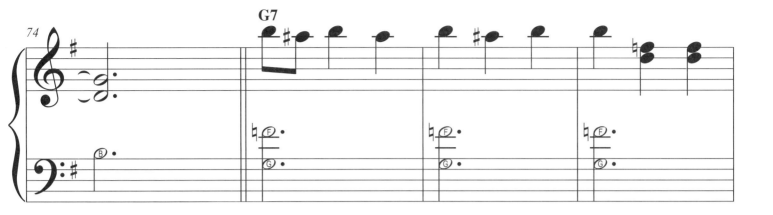

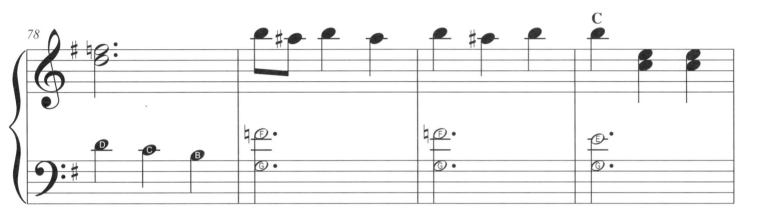

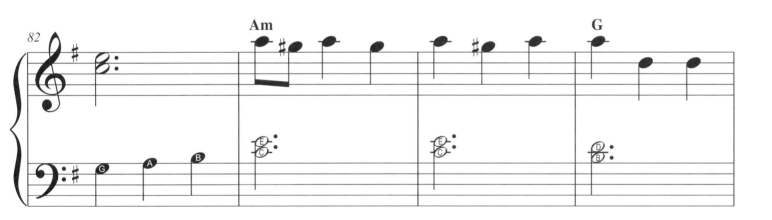

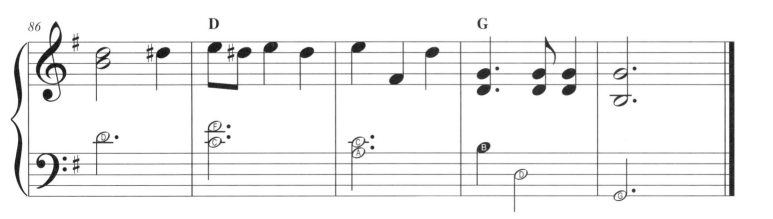

# TOYLAND

This arrangement helps you create a charming music-box effect. Before you play, however, there are several things you should take note of in your music:

- Throughout the arrangement, the melody is played an octave higher than written.
- The entire left-hand part appears on a treble staff. This allows you to play the accompaniment more easily on a higher-sounding part of the keyboard. Letter-names are included to guide you.
- The accompaniment includes several different playing styles – broken chords, pyramid chords, and single notes. Be sure to practice this part alone before you play the entire song.
- You might also want to practice the right hand alone in measures 13 and 14.
- In measure 31, you'll see the marking *rit.* This is an abbreviation for *ritardando*, an Italian word that means to "gradually slow down." As you play the notes in the arpeggio, you can create the effect of a music box running down.
- Fermatas appear in measures 28 and 32.
- Be sure to observe the suggested fingering.

# TOYLAND
## from BABES IN TOYLAND

Words by Glen MacDonough
Music by Victor Herbert

**Key: F major**

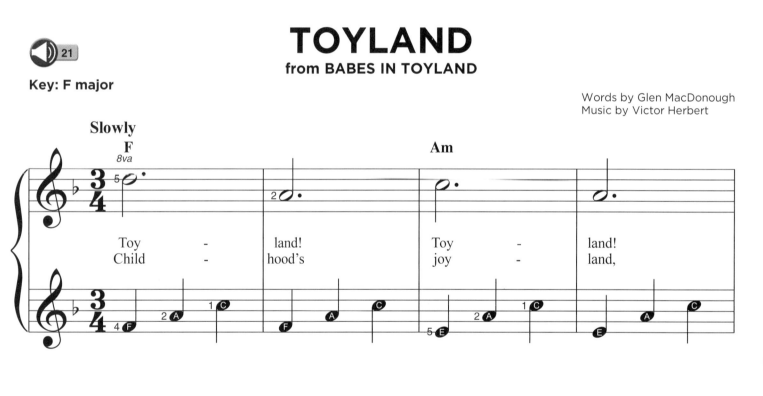

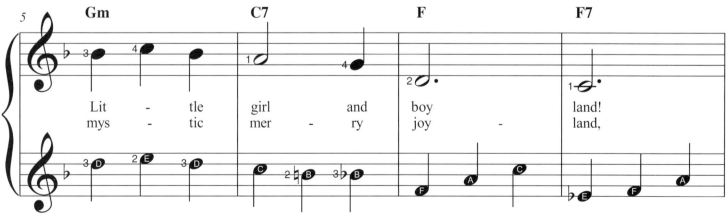

While you dwell with - in it, \_\_\_\_\_ you are
once you pass its

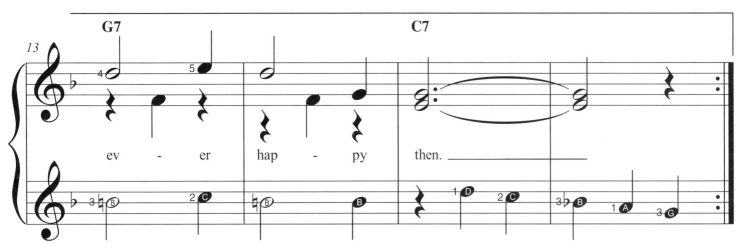

ev - er hap - py then. \_\_\_\_\_

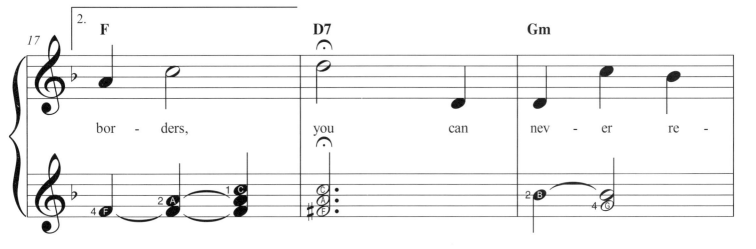

bor - ders, you can nev - er re -

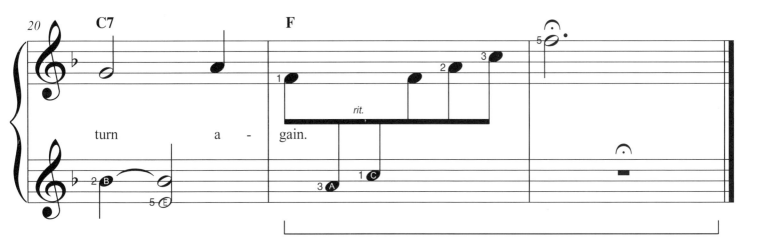

turn a - gain.

## EIGHTH-NOTE TRIPLETS

A triplet is a group of three notes played in the same amount of time it would take to play two notes of the same type. It's easy to recognize the triplet because the three notes usually have the number 3 over the middle one.

The illustration shows how all the eighth-note triplets should be counted in relation to other types of notes. Start by tapping your foot slowly and saying the words; then tap your foot and play in the same rhythm as the lyric.

Jin-gle bells, won-der-ful sound.

Practice the exercise shown below.

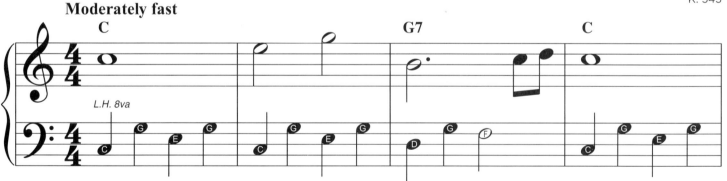

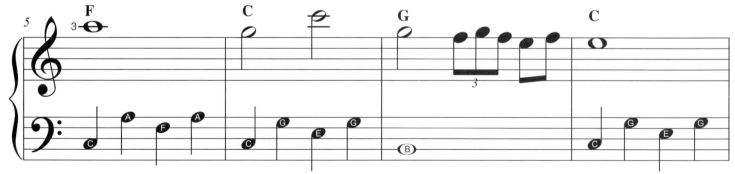

# SONATA IN C MAJOR

**Key: C major**

By Wolfgang Amadeus Mozart
K. 545

**Moderately fast**

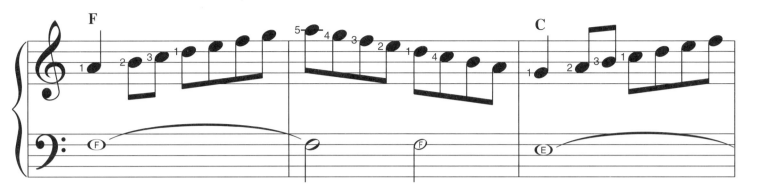

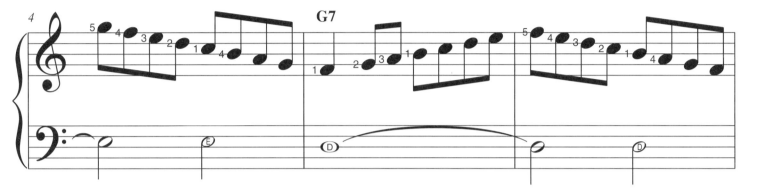

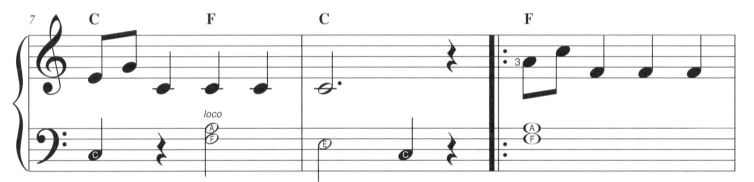

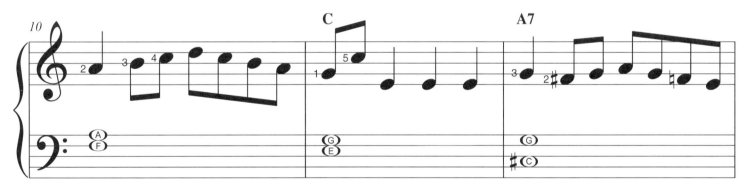

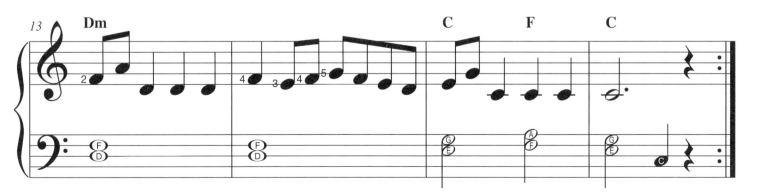

## 16TH NOTES

The time value of a *16th note* is one-half that of an eighth note and one-fourth that of a quarter note. You already know each beat can be divided into two equal parts – a number and the word "and."

When you count 16th notes, each beat may be divided into four equal parts. Each part is indicated by a separate syllable. Play the example slowly while counting aloud and tapping your foot. Play four 16th notes to each foot tap. Make sure you can play them evenly and without hesitation.

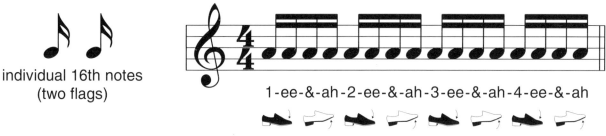

individual 16th notes
(two flags)

1-ee-&-ah-2-ee-&-ah-3-ee-&-ah-4-ee-&-ah

## DOTTED-EIGHTH AND 16TH NOTES

Since an eighth note has a time value of one half-beat, a dot after an eighth note adds one half of that time value (one-fourth-beat) to it. Therefore, the total time value of a *dotted-eighth note* equals three-fourths of one beat.

When a dotted-eighth note occurs in music, it is usually followed by a *16th note*. The combined value of these two notes is equivalent to one beat. When this combination of notes appears on a song sheet, the stems are connected by a beam, and the 16th note has a small bar attached to its stem, representing the second flag.

A complete measure in 4/4 time, containing the dotted-eighth-note/16th-note pattern is counted as shown. The effect is similar to a gallop.

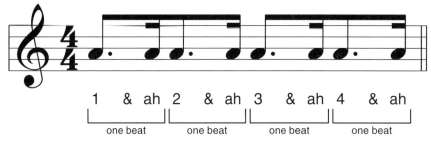

## QUARTER-NOTE TRIPLETS

Earlier, you learned that eighth-note triplets are played in the same time it takes to play two notes of the same type. This same principle applies to quarter-note triplets, which have the same time value as two quarter notes; that is, two beats.

The figure shows how to count quarter-note triplets. While tapping your foot in a slow, even tempo, and counting aloud, play the first measure. When you reach the second measure, play the first note on the first downbeat (foot tap).

Here's a rule to remember: The first note of a quarter-note triplet is *always* played on the beat. The second note is played just before, and the third note is just played after, the second beat.

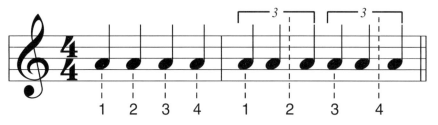

# OTHER TIME SIGNATURES

All the music you've played up to now has had a time signature of either 3/4 or 4/4. There are many other time signatures used in music, however. 6/8 means there are six beats in each measure and every eighth note gets one beat. The natural accents are on beats 1 and 4. 3/8 means three beats in every measure and an eighth note gets one beat. This is counted the same as 3/4 time, with the natural accent on beat 1.

With an 8 on the bottom of a time signature, an eighth note gets one beat, a quarter note gets two beats, a dotted-quarter note gets three beats, and a dotted-half note gets six beats, etc.

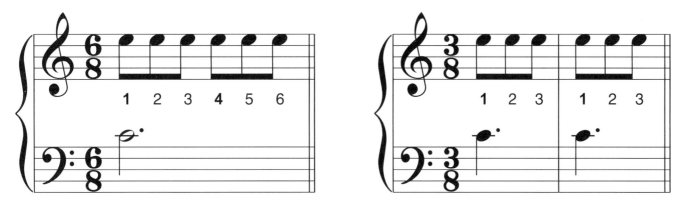

# MUSIC GLOSSARY

Most of the following are either traditional markings to help add expression to your playing, or standard musical definitions.

**a tempo:** Return to the original tempo.

**accelerando:** Increase the tempo; speed up.

**accent:** To emphasize or stress a note; indicated by the symbol ( > ).

**arpeggio:** Symbol ( 〳 ) appearing before a chord that tells you to play one note at a time, from lowest to highest.

**crescendo** (*cresc.* or ⟨‾‾‾ ): Become gradually louder.

**da capo** (*D.C.*)**:** "From the beginning;" a type of repeat.

**da capo al fine** (*D.C. al Fine*)**:** Repeat from the beginning to the Fine indication.

**dal segno** (*D.S.*)**:** "From the sign" 𝄋; a type of repeat.

**dal segno al fine** (*D.S. al Fine*)**:** Repeat from the sign 𝄋 to the end (Fine).

**dal segno al coda** (*D.S. al Coda*)**:** Repeat from the sign 𝄋 to where the To Coda ⊕ sign appears; go straight to the Coda.

**diminuendo** (*dim.* or ‾‾‾⟩ ): Become gradually softer.

**dolce:** "Sweetly." An indication to play sweetly and smoothly (legato).

**double bar:** Two vertical lines appearing at the end of a section.

**double flat** ♭♭ **:** Lowers a tone two half steps.

**double sharp** 𝄪 **:** Raises a tone two half steps.

**dynamics:** Contrasts in volume.

*pp* – *pianissimo*; very soft      *mf* – *mezzo forte*; moderately loud

*p* – *piano*; soft      *f* – *forte*; loud

*mp* – *mezzo piano*; moderately soft      *ff* – *fortissimo*; very loud

**enharmonic tones:** Tones having the same pitch, but notated differently; e.g., F♯ and G♭.

**expression:** Your own touch added to music by variations in volume, touch, and sometimes tempo.

**espressivo:** With expression.

**fermata** ⌒ **:** A sign indicating that a note is to be held longer than its notated time value.

**final bar line:** A thick double bar appearing at the end of a song.

**fine:** Italian term meaning "the end;" pronounced *fee-nay*.

**glissando** ⟋ **:** Sliding rapidly from one key to another, playing all keys between.

**grandioso:** Grandiose, grandly.

**interval:** The distance between two notes.

**legato:** Smoothly.

**loco:** Play at the indicated pitch; cancels 8va/8vb.

**maestoso:** Majestically, stately.

**modulate:** To change key signatures within a song.

**notes:** The written symbols of music.

**octave:** An interval of eight notes.

**octave higher:** Symbol *8va* or *8va - - - ⌐* placed above the music, indicating that notes should be played one octave higher than written.

**octave lower:** Symbol *8vb* or *8vb - - - ⌐* placed below the music, indicating that notes should be played one octave lower than written.

**pause** ⫽ **:** A brief break in the music.

**pitch:** The highness or lowness of a note.

**poco a poco:** Little by little; gradually.

**portato:** Slightly disconnected notes.

**rallentando** (*rall.*)**:** Becoming gradually slower.

**ritardando** (*rit.*)**:** Same as rallentando.

**rubato:** Freely slowing down and speeding up the tempo without changing the basic pulse; Italian term for "robbed."

**sempre:** Always.

**sforzando** (*sfz*)**:** A strong, heavy accent on a note; stronger than ＞ .

**simile:** Play in a similar manner.

**slur:** A curved line connecting two or more notes, indicating that they should be played *legato.*

**staccato:** "Detatched." Short, separated notes indicated.

**tempo:** "Time." The pace of a piece of music.

### Common Tempo Markings

largo – very slowly and broadly.

lento – slowly.

adagio – slowly, but not as slow as lento.

andante – "going;" a moderate, graceful tempo.

moderato – medium, moderate speed.

allegretto – a light, cheerful, fast tempo; a bit slower than allegro.

allegro – "cheerful;" a lively, fast tempo.

presto – very fast.

vivace – lively, brisk, quick, bright.

**tone:** A note, the basis of music.

# CHORD CHART
## CHORDS USED IN PART 2

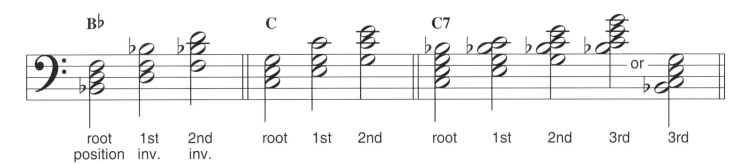

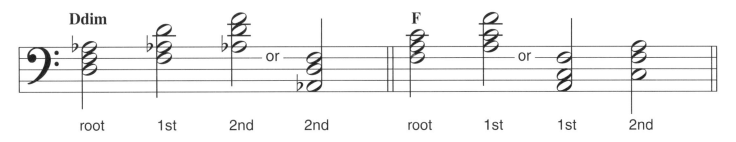

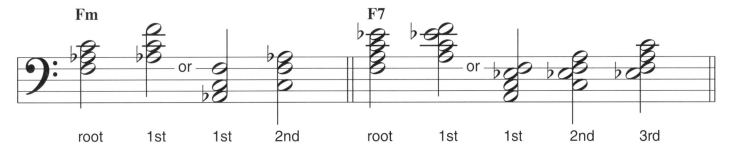

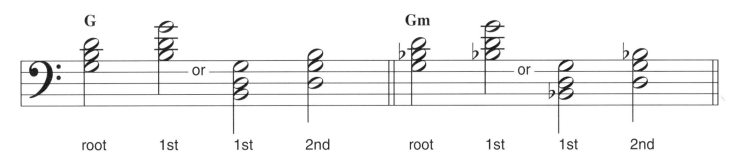

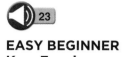

**EASY BEGINNER**
**Key: F major**

# AULD LANG SYNE

Words by Robert Burns
Traditional Scottish Melody

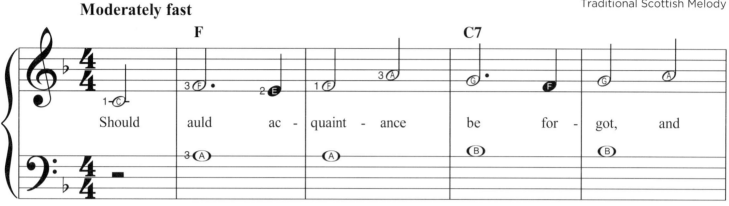

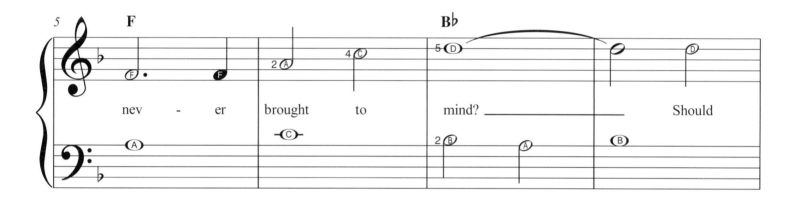

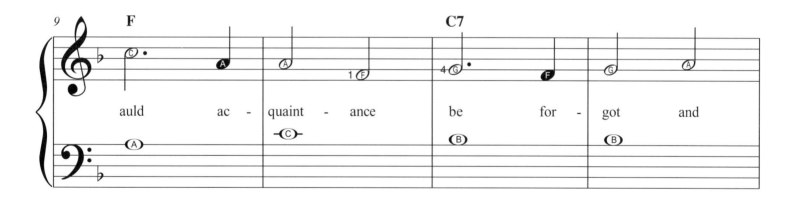

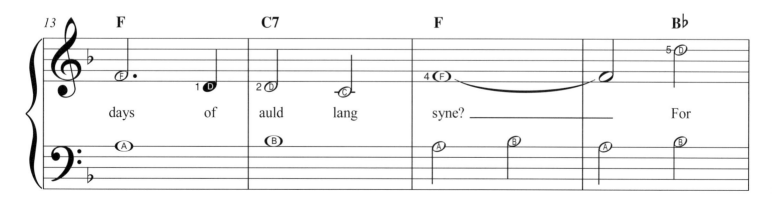

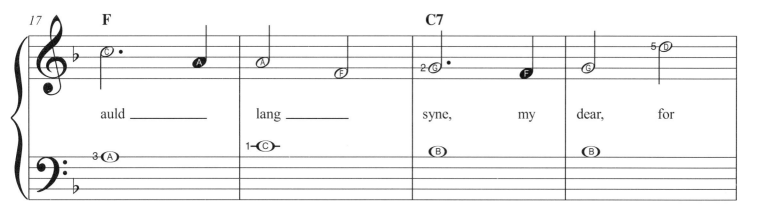

auld _____ lang _____ syne, my dear, for

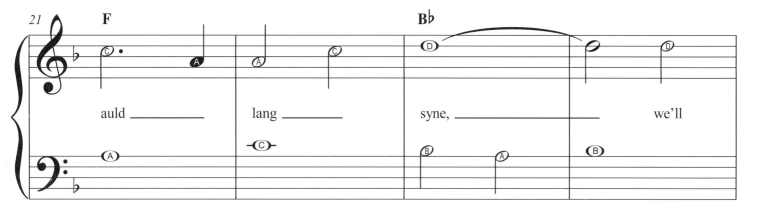

auld _____ lang _____ syne, _____ we'll

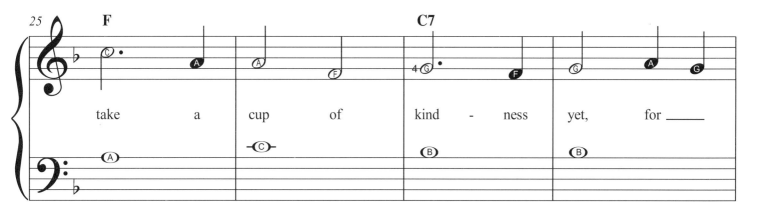

take a cup of kind - ness yet, for _____

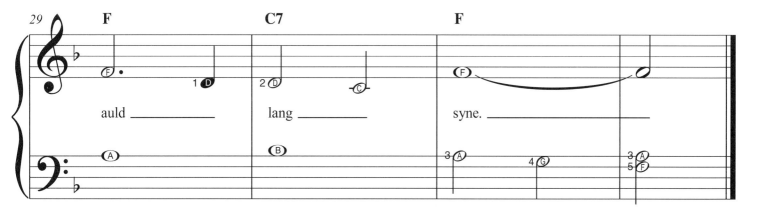

auld _____ lang _____ syne. _____

# AULD LANG SYNE

Words by Robert Burns
Traditional Scottish Melody

**Moderately fast**

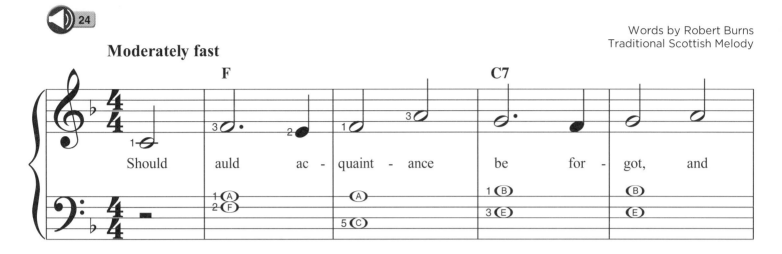

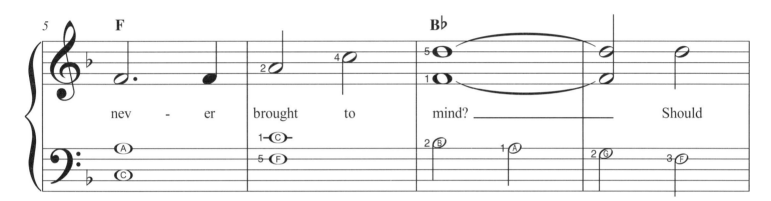

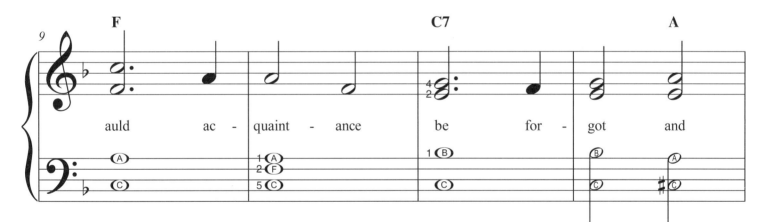

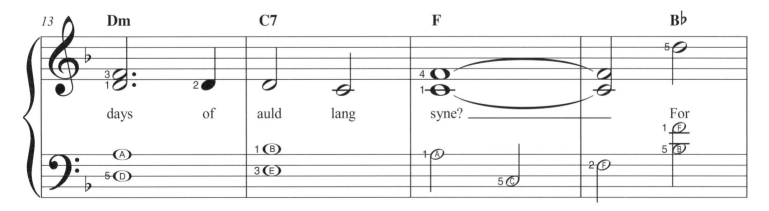

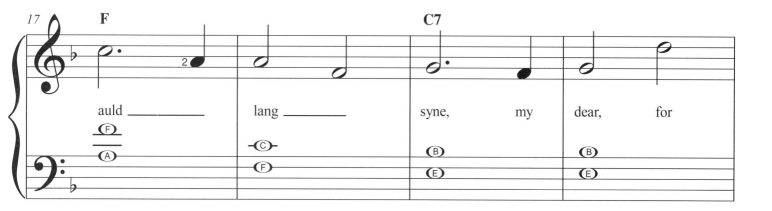

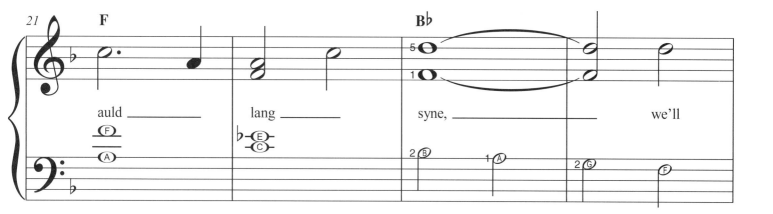

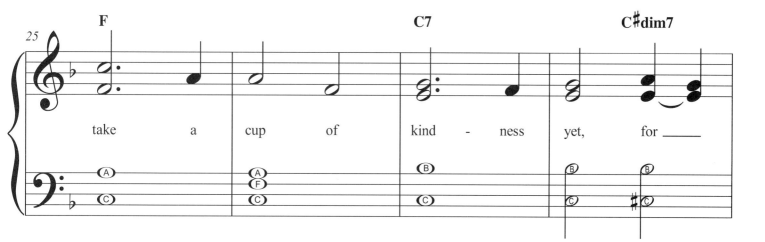

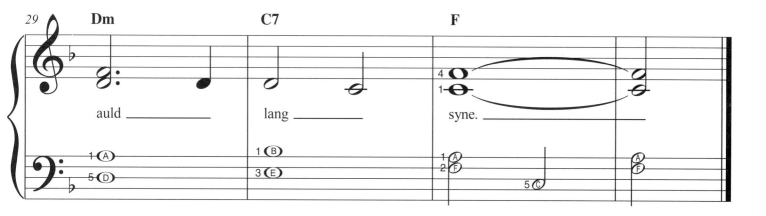

# JINGLE BELLS

Words and Music by
J. Pierpont

**Moderately fast**

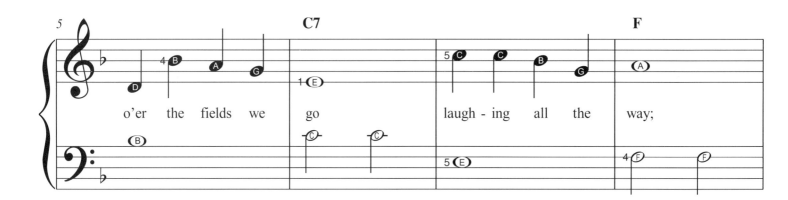

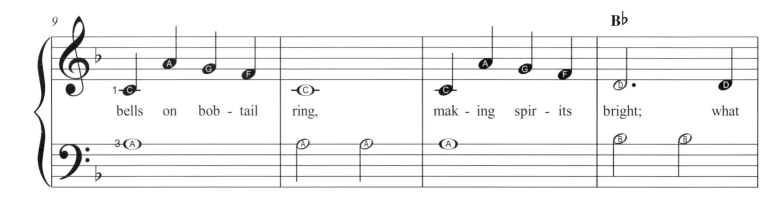

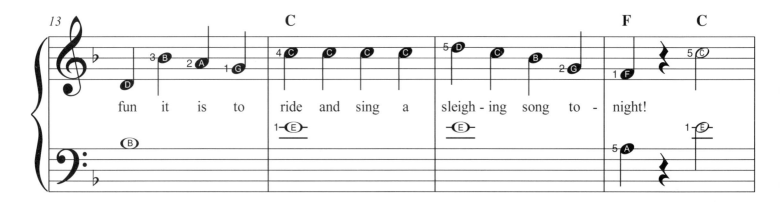

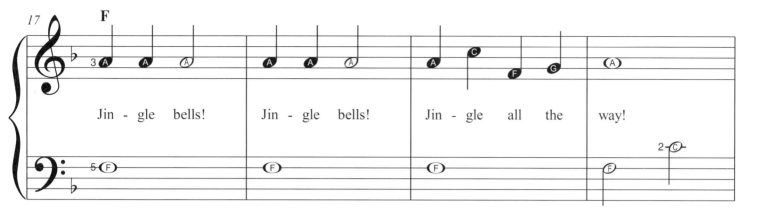

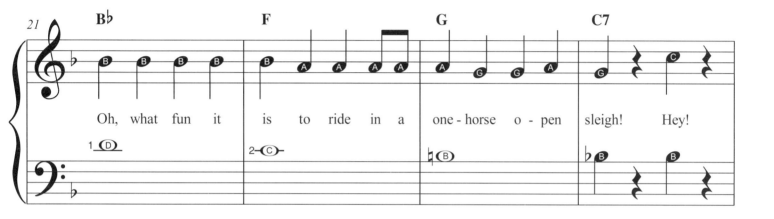

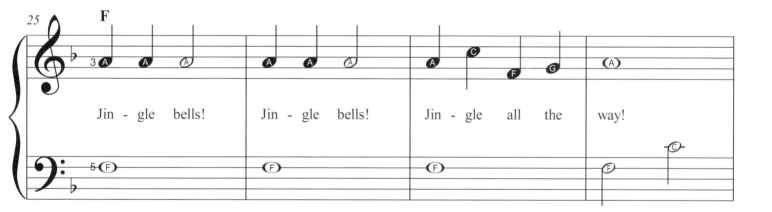

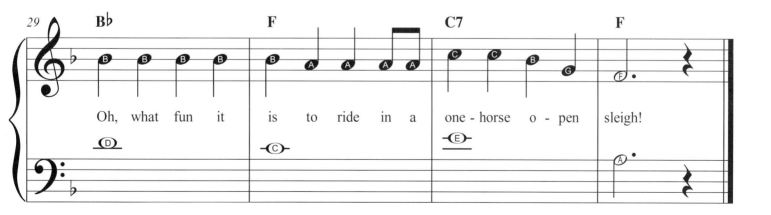

91

# JINGLE BELLS

Words and Music by
J. Pierpont

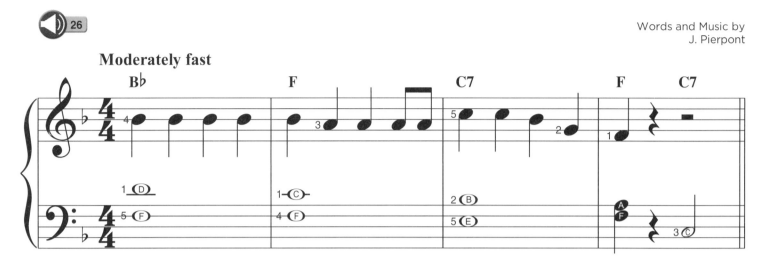

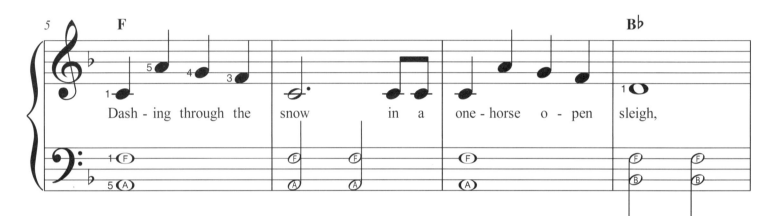

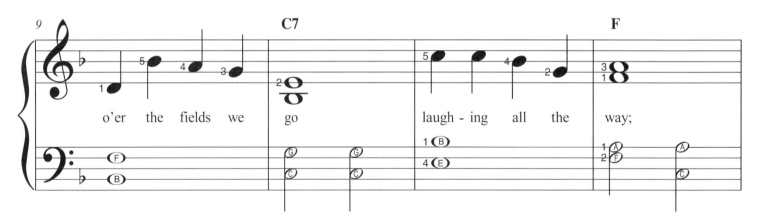

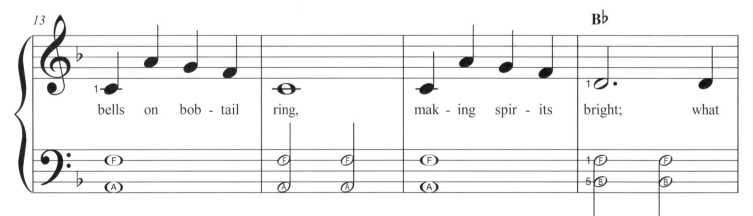

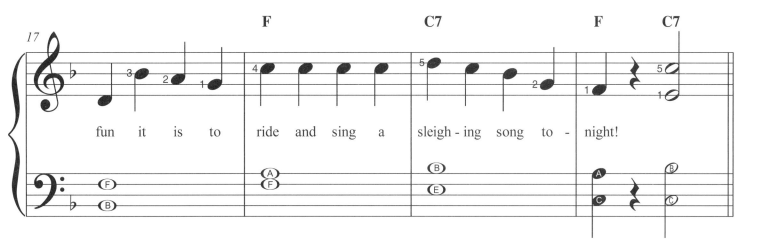

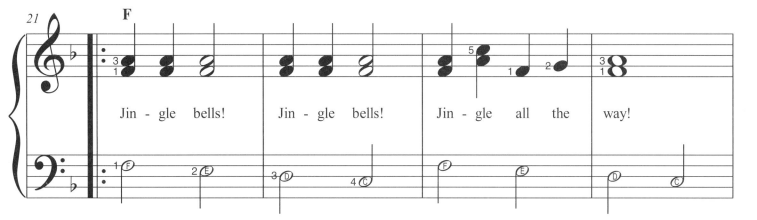

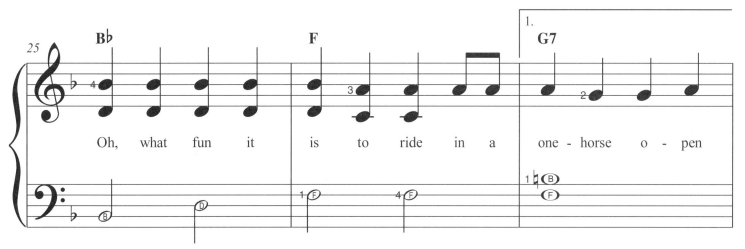

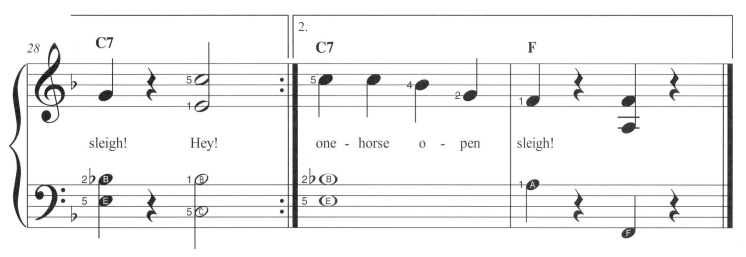

**EASY BEGINNER**
**Key: F major**

# HARK! THE HERALD ANGELS SING

Words by Charles Wesley
Music by Felix Mendelssohn

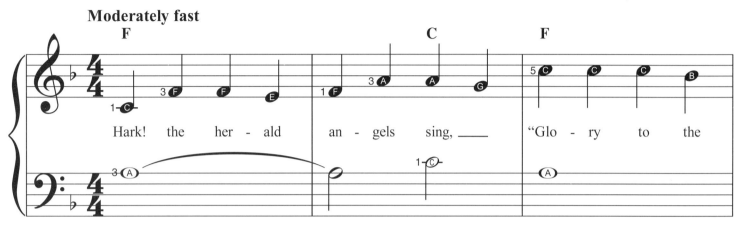

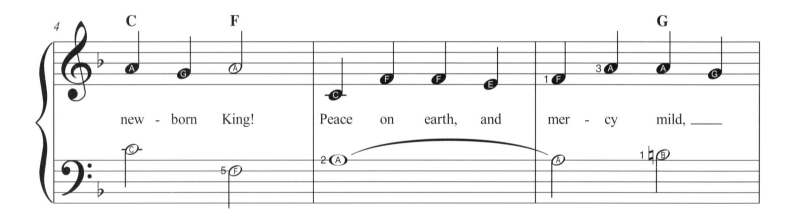

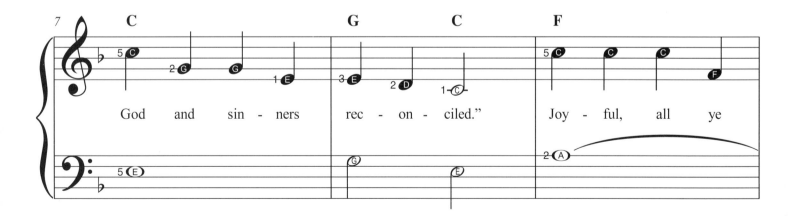

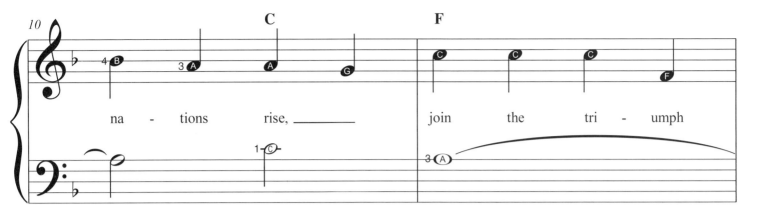

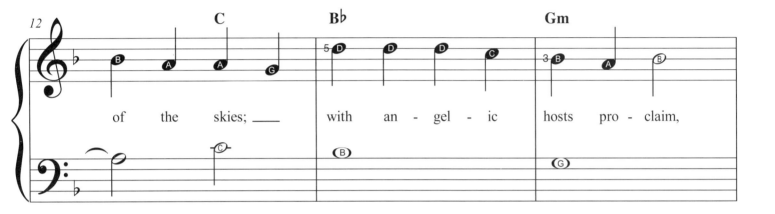

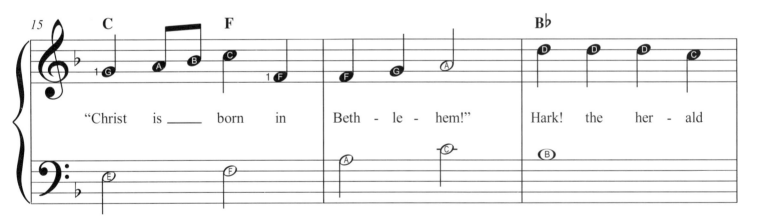

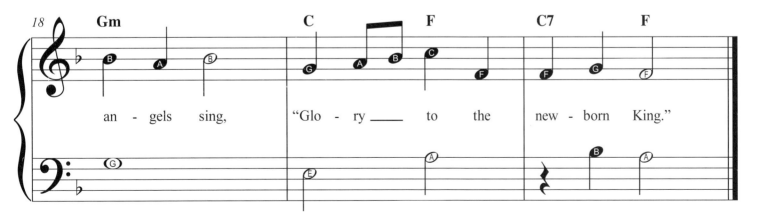

# HARK! THE HERALD ANGELS SING

Words by Charles Wesley
Music by Felix Mendelssohn

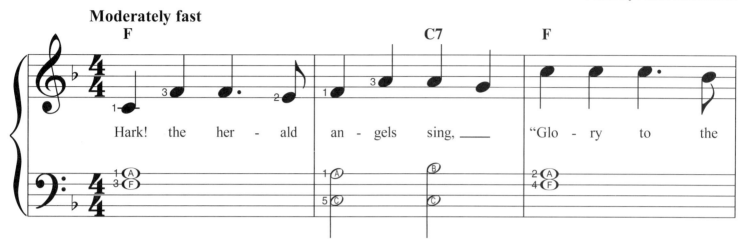

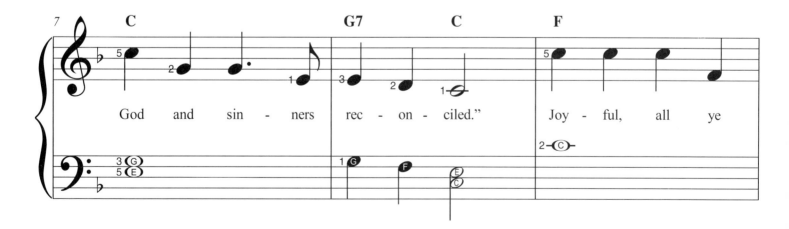

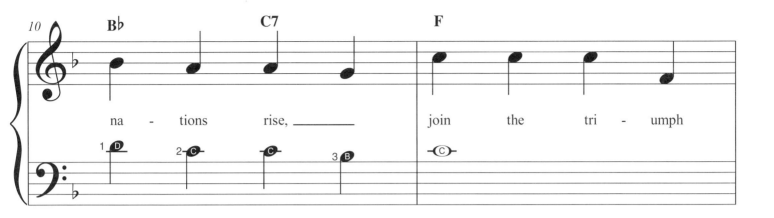

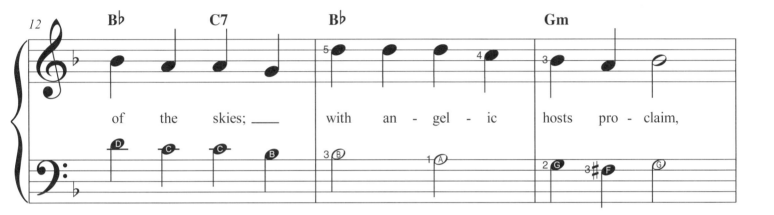

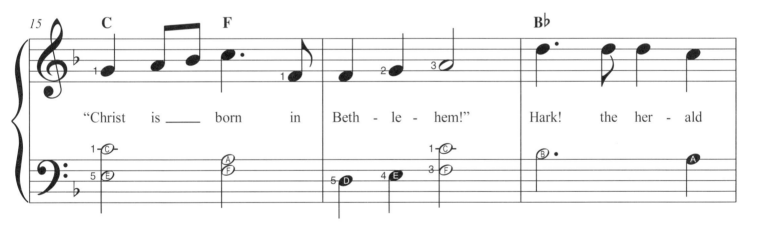

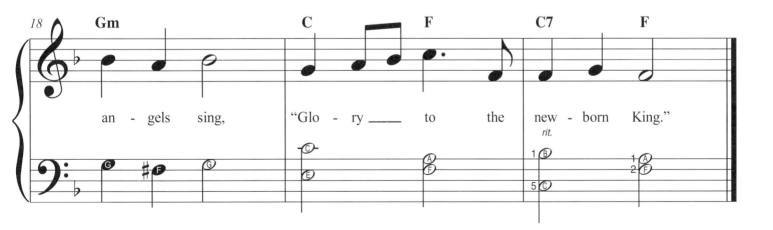

**EASY BEGINNER**
**Key: C major**

# SILENT NIGHT

Words by Joseph Mohr
Music by Franz X. Gruber

**Slowly and gently**

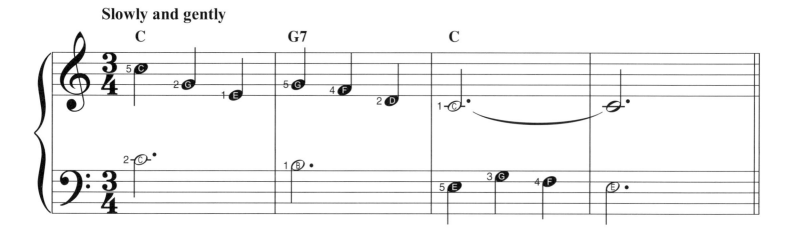

Si - lent night, ho - ly night!

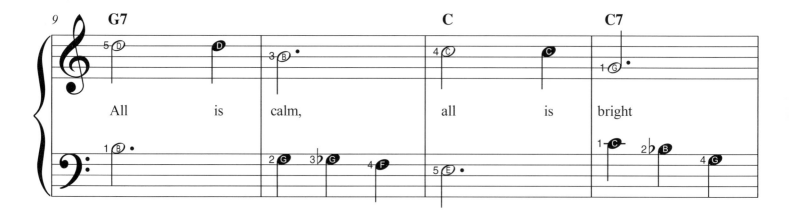

All is calm, all is bright

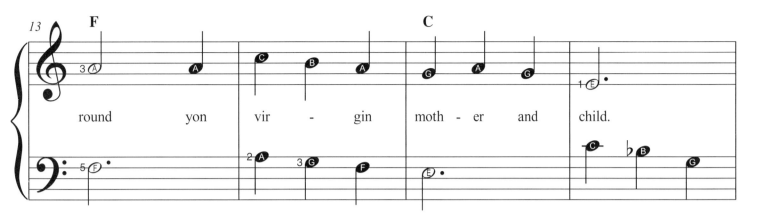

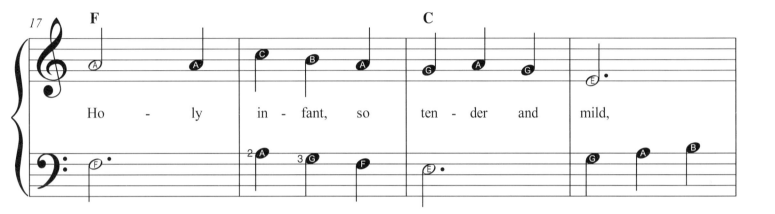

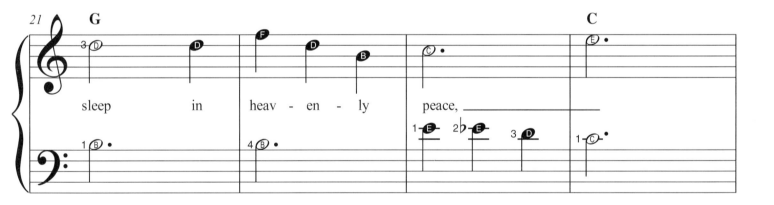

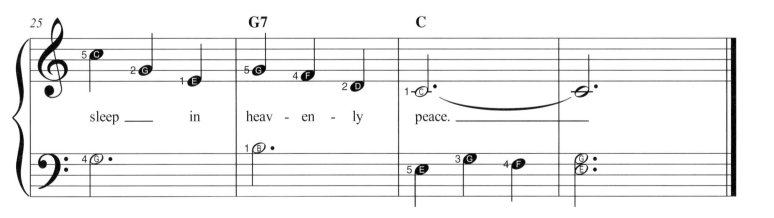

# SILENT NIGHT

Words by Joseph Mohr
Music by Franz X. Gruber

**Slowly and gently**

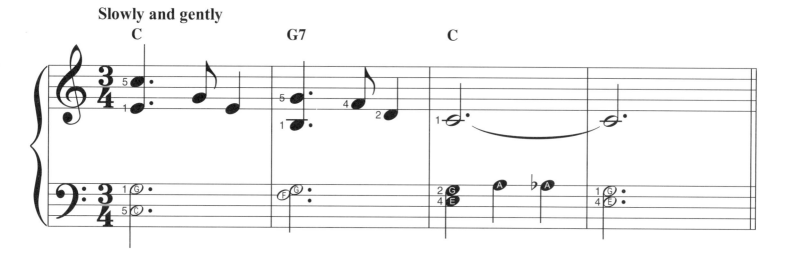

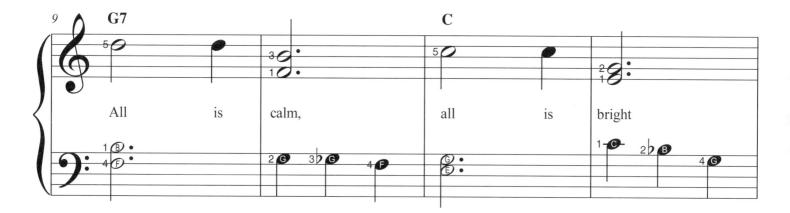

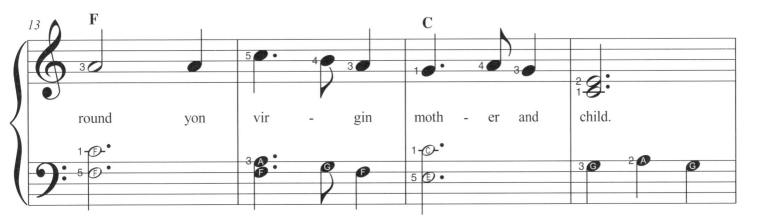

round     yon     vir -   gin     moth - er  and     child.

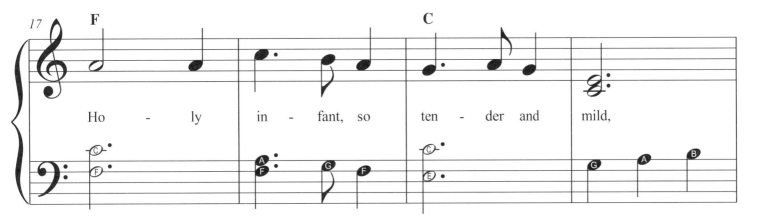

Ho -   ly     in - fant, so    ten - der and     mild,

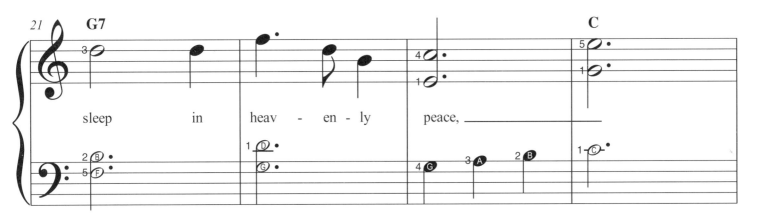

sleep     in    heav - en - ly     peace, _____

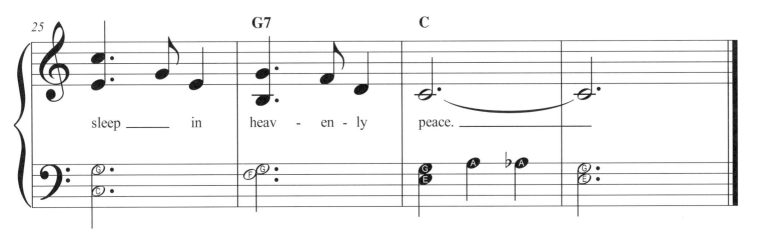

sleep _____ in    heav - en - ly     peace. _____

# BEAUTIFUL BROWN EYES

**EASY BEGINNER**
**Key: C major**

Traditional

🔊 31

**Slowly and tenderly**

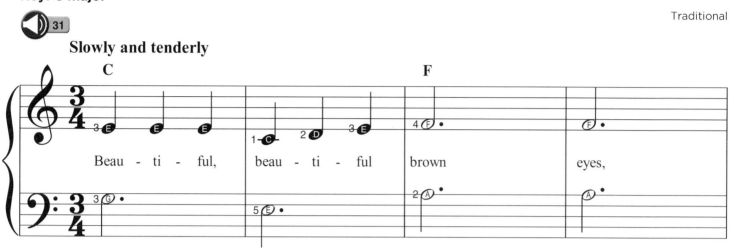

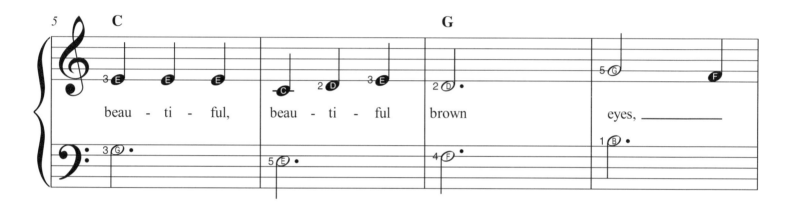

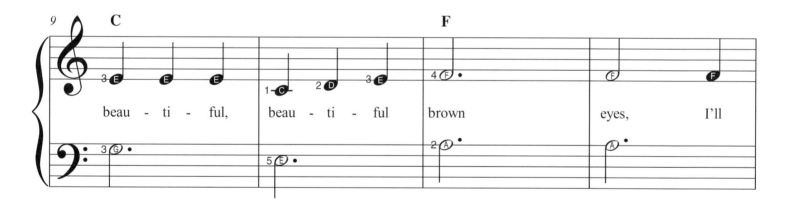

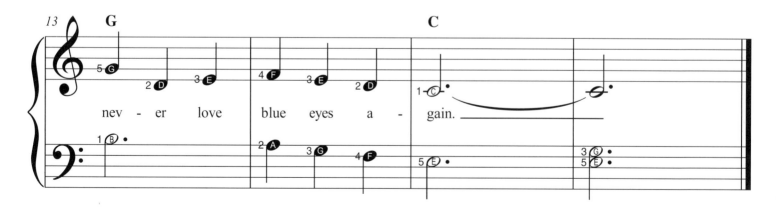

# BEAUTIFUL BROWN EYES

**EASY PRO**
**Key: C major**

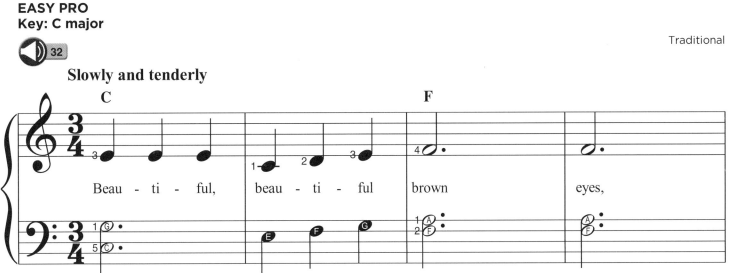

Traditional

**Slowly and tenderly**

Beau - ti - ful, beau - ti - ful brown eyes,

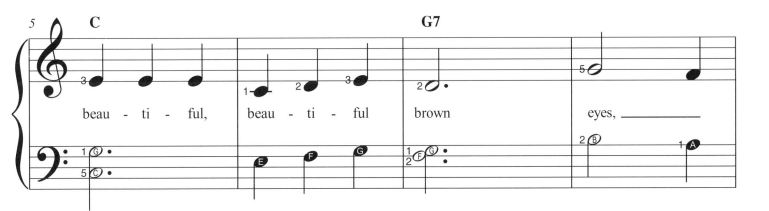

beau - ti - ful, beau - ti - ful brown eyes, _____

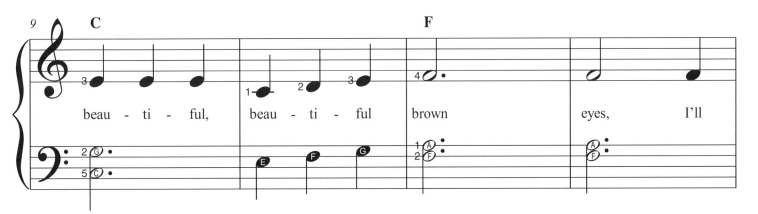

beau - ti - ful, beau - ti - ful brown eyes, I'll

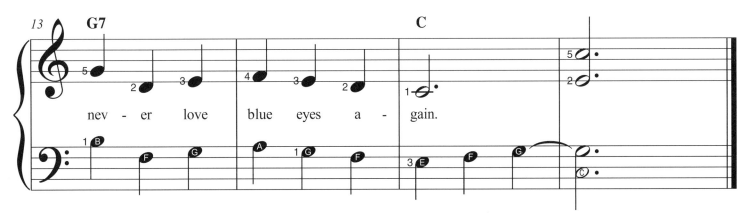

nev - er love blue eyes a - gain.

# NEW WORLD SYMPHONY

**EASY BEGINNER**
**Key: C major**

**(Theme)**

By Antonin Dvořák
Op. 95

**Slowly**

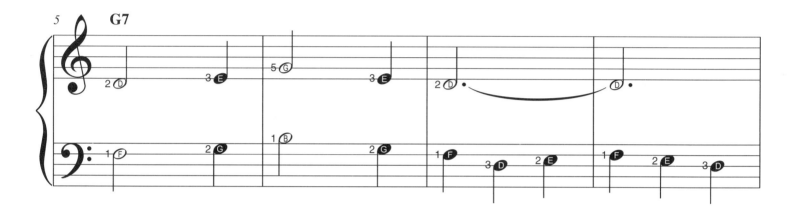

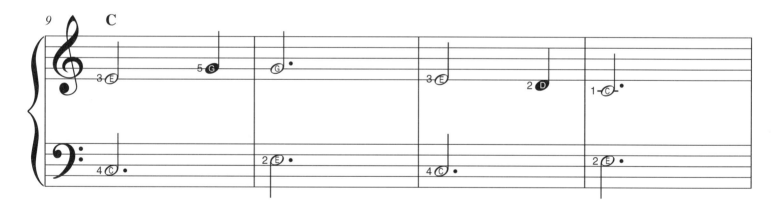

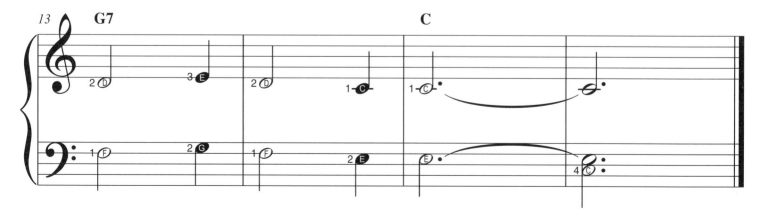

# NEW WORLD SYMPHONY

## (Theme)

**EASY PRO**
**Key: C major**

By Antonin Dvořák
Op. 95

**Slowly**

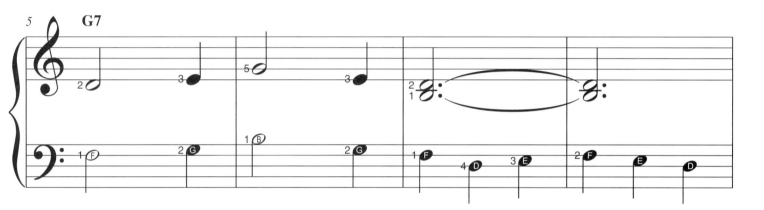

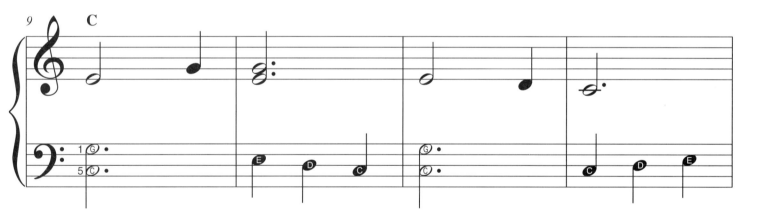

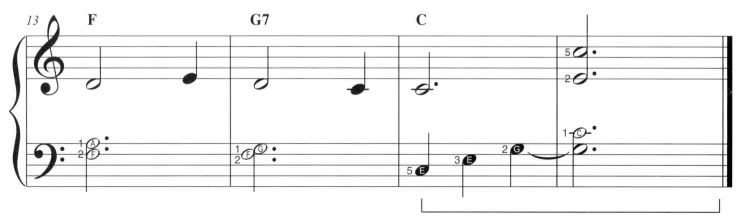

# BARCAROLLE
**from THE TALES OF HOFFMANN**

By Jacques Offenbach

**Moderate Waltz**

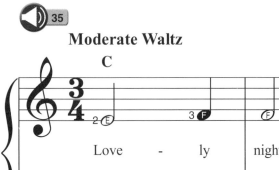

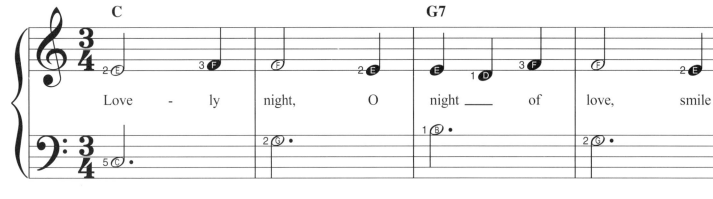

Love - ly night, O night ___ of love, smile

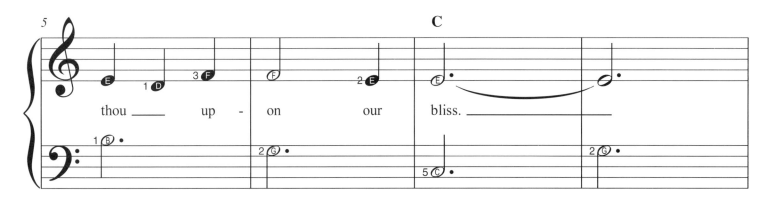

thou ___ up - on our bliss. ___

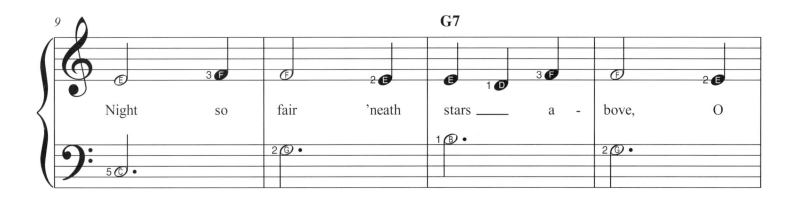

Night so fair 'neath stars ___ a - bove, O

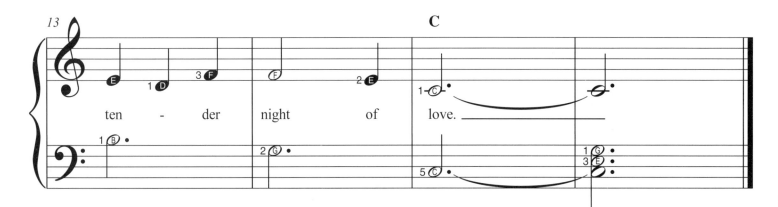

ten - der night of love. ___

# BARCAROLLE
## from THE TALES OF HOFFMANN

By Jacques Offenbach

**Moderate Waltz**

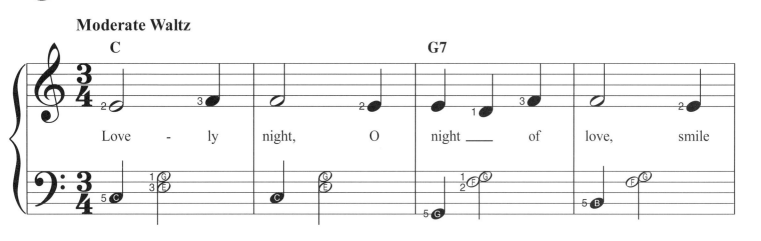

Love - ly night, O night ___ of love, smile

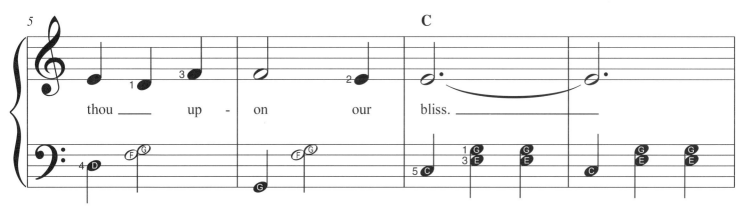

thou ___ up - on our bliss. ___

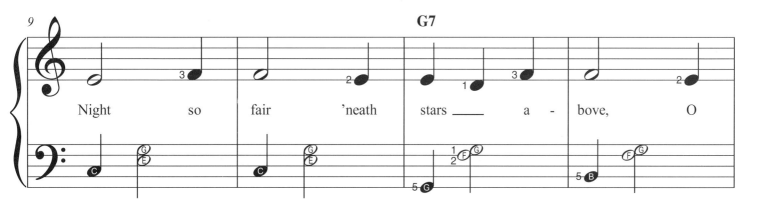

Night so fair 'neath stars ___ a - bove, O

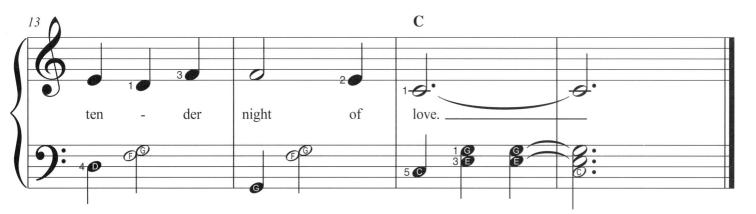

ten - der night of love. ___

# LONG, LONG AGO

By Thomas Bayly

**Moderately slow**

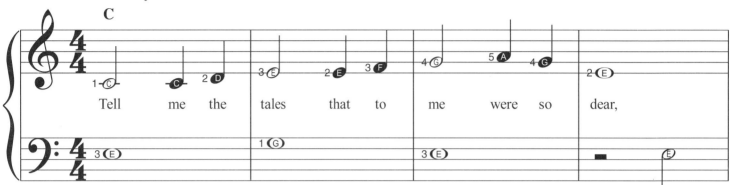

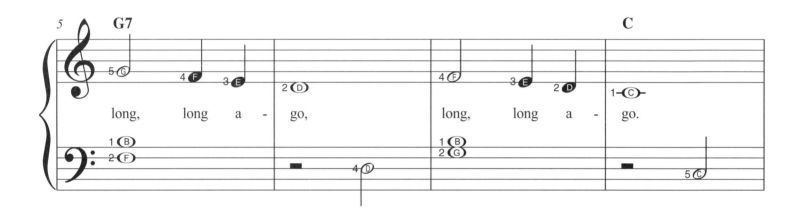

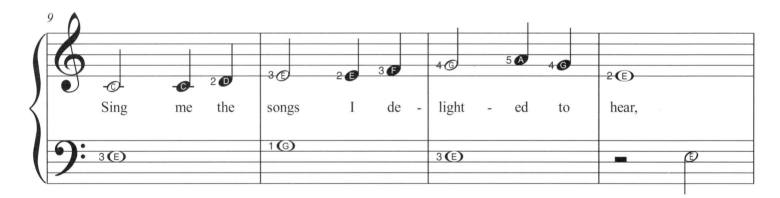

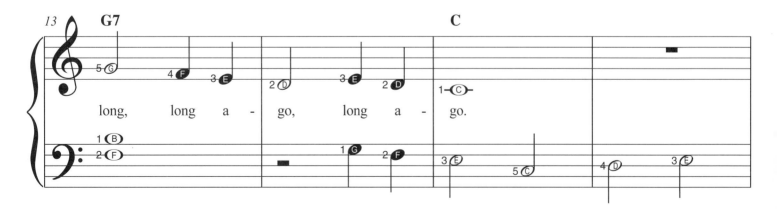

Now you are here all my grief is re - moved.

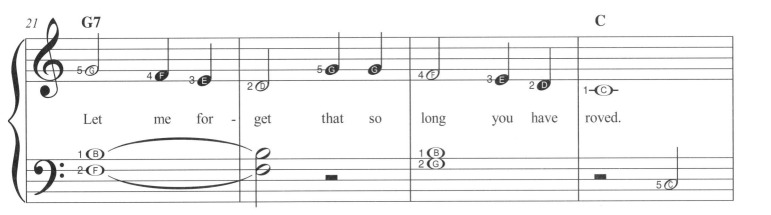

Let me for - get that so long you have roved.

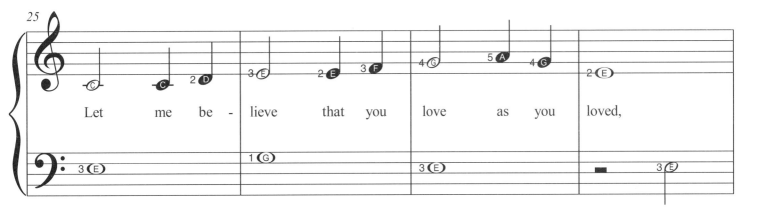

Let me be - lieve that you love as you loved,

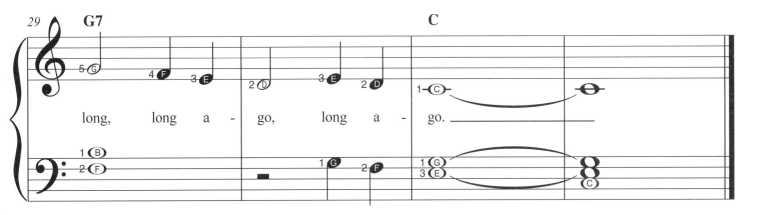

long, long a - go, long a - go.

# LONG, LONG AGO

By Thomas Bayly

**Moderately slow**

Tell me the tales that to me were so dear,

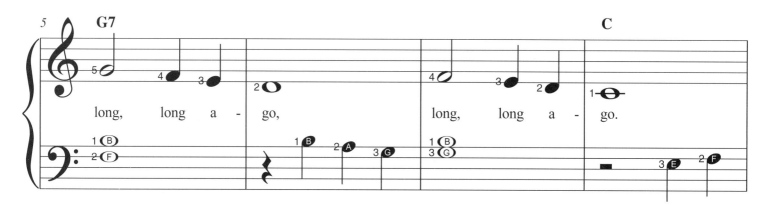

long, long a - go, long, long a - go.

Sing me the songs I de - light - ed to hear,

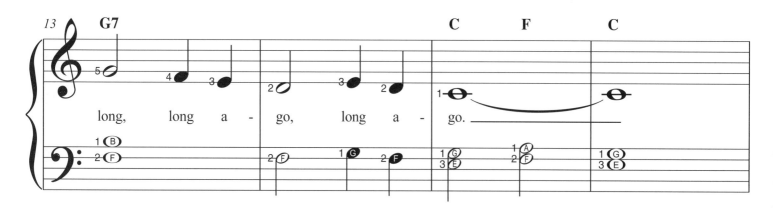

long, long a - go, long a - go.

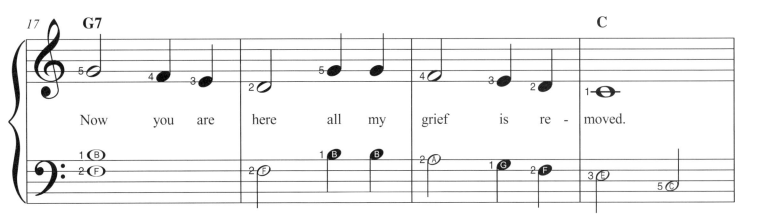

Now you are here all my grief is re - moved.

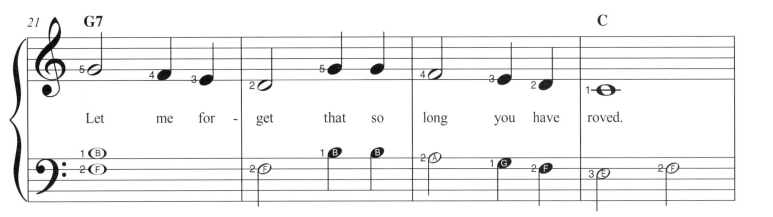

Let me for - get that so long you have roved.

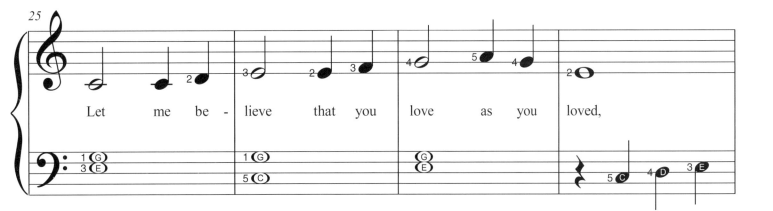

Let me be - lieve that you love as you loved,

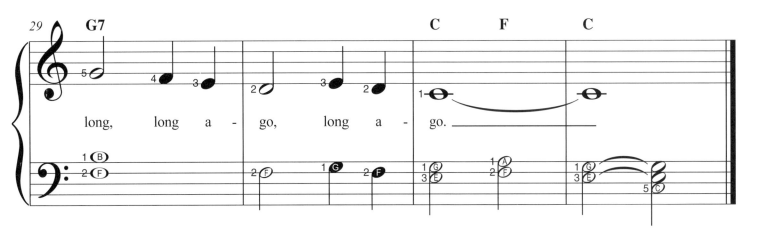

long, long a - go, long a - go.

**EASY BEGINNER**
**Key: G major**

# AURA LEE

Words by W.W. Fosdick
Music by George R. Poulton

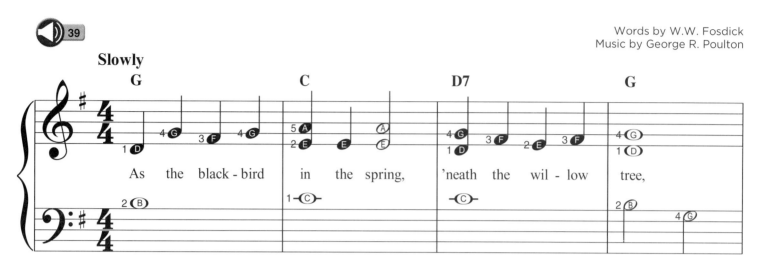

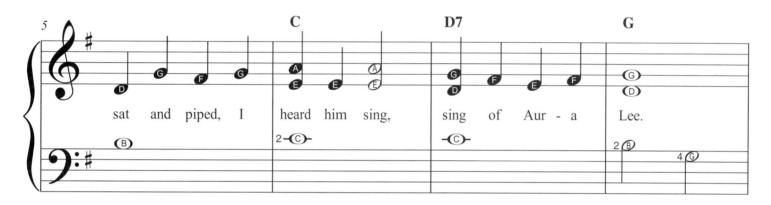

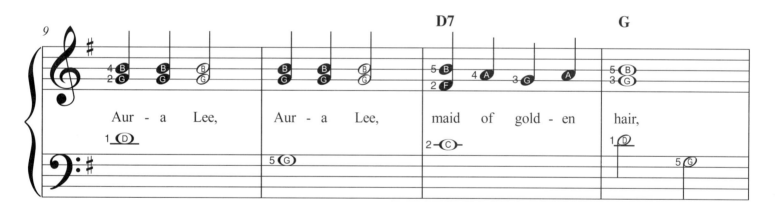

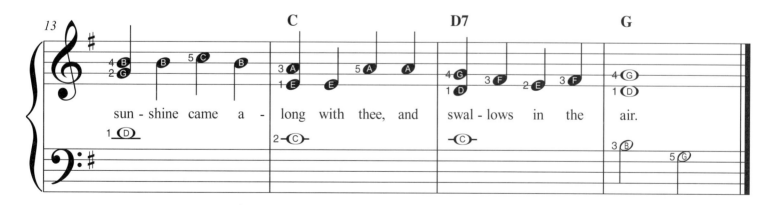

# AURA LEE

Words by W.W. Fosdick
Music by George R. Poulton

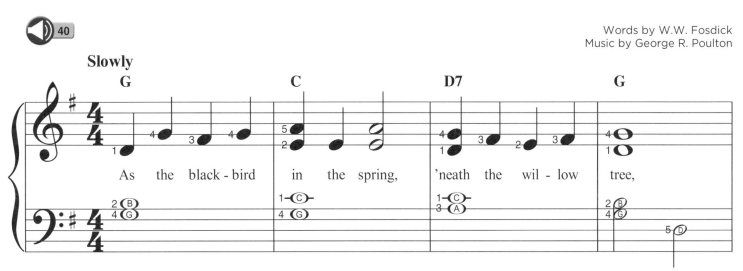

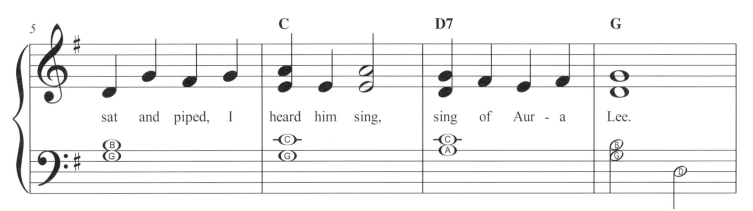

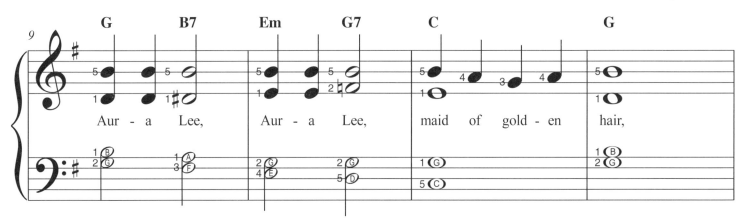

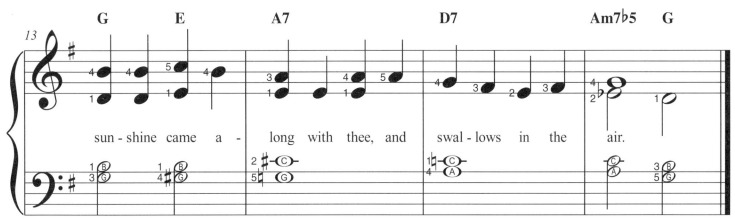

**EASY BEGINNER**
Key: G major

# AMAZING GRACE

Words by John Newton
Traditional American Melody

**Moderately slow**

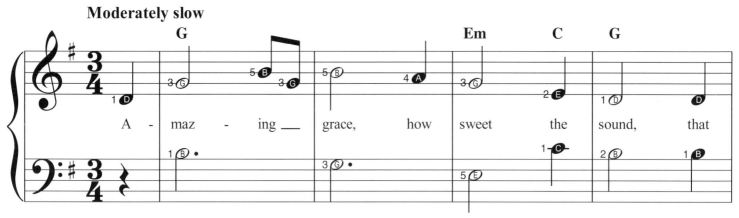

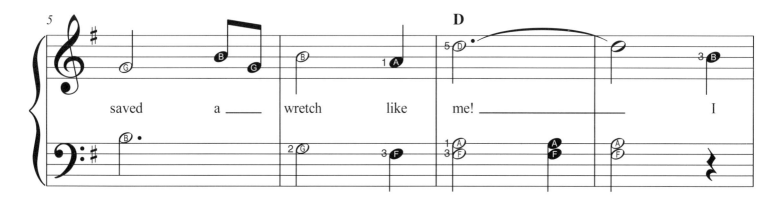

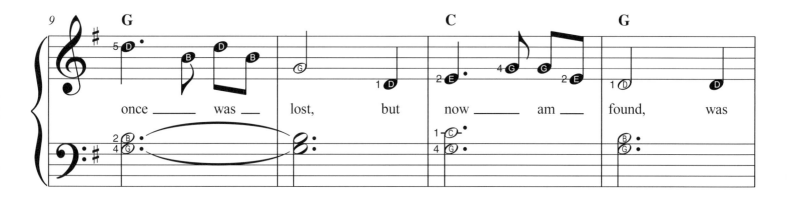

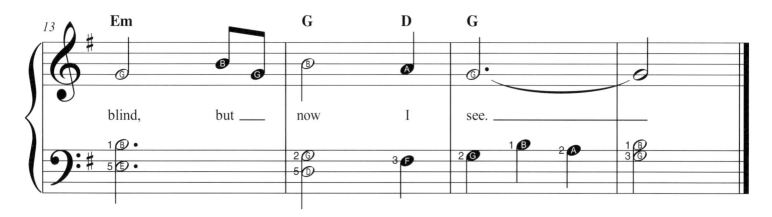

# AMAZING GRACE

Words by John Newton
Traditional American Melody

Moderately slow

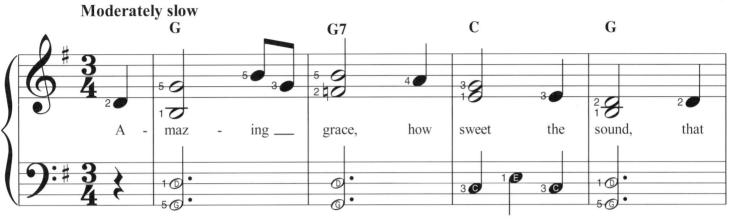

A - maz - ing ___ grace, how sweet the sound, that

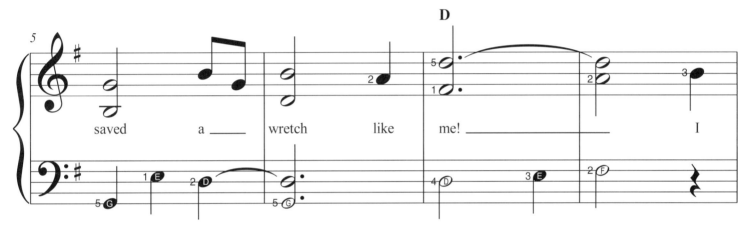

saved a ___ wretch like me! ___ I

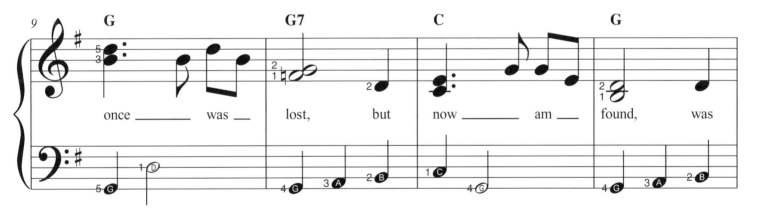

once ___ was ___ lost, but now ___ am ___ found, was

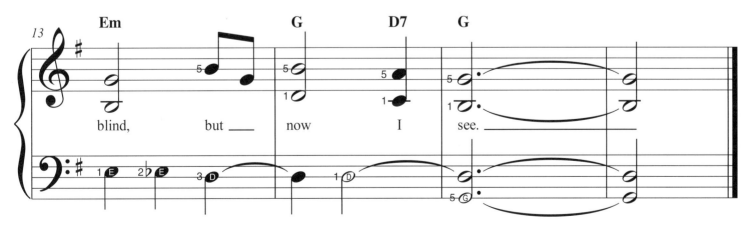

blind, but ___ now I see. ___

# I LOVE YOU TRULY

Words and Music by
CARRIE JACOBS-BOND

**Moderately slow**

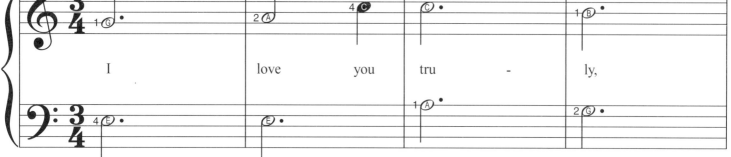

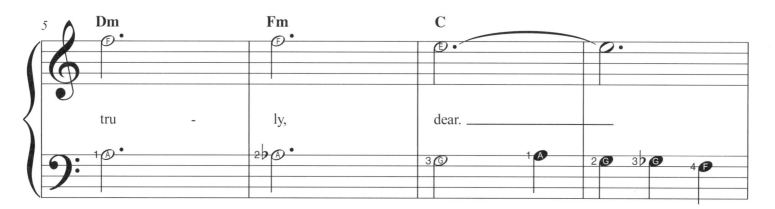

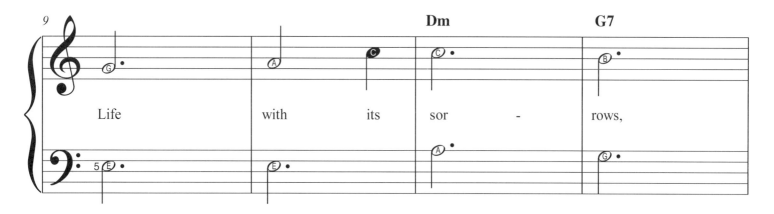

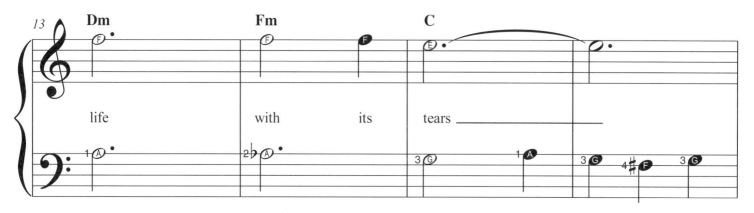

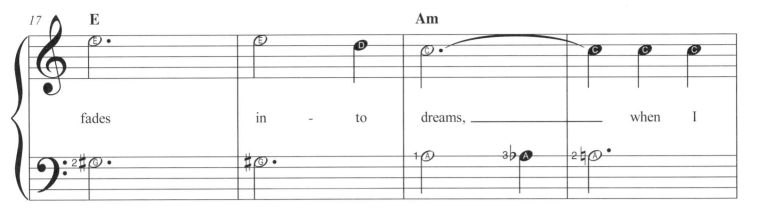

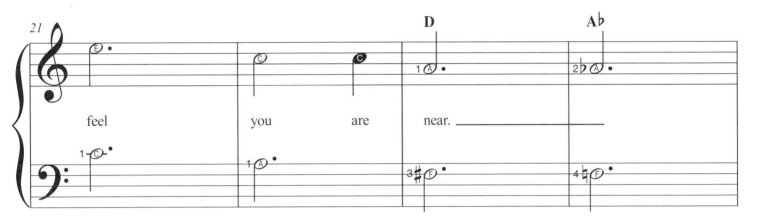

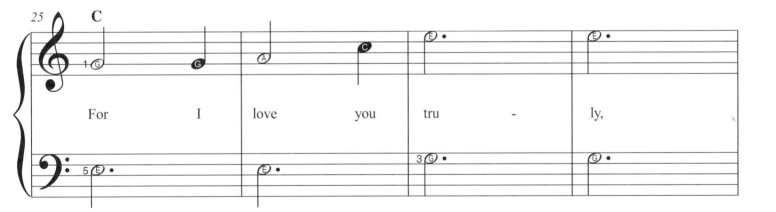

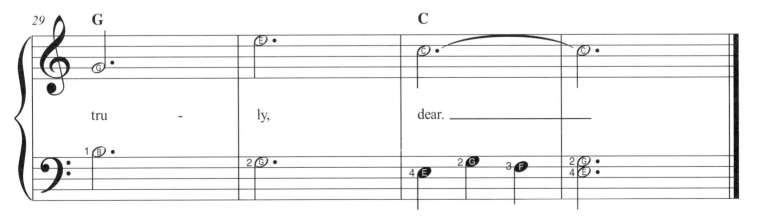

EASY PRO
Key: C Major

# I LOVE YOU TRULY

Words and Music by
CARRIE JACOBS-BOND

Moderately slow

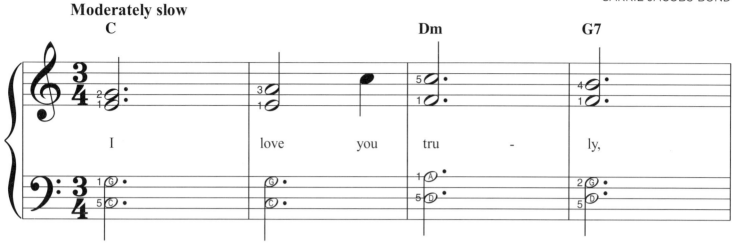

I love you tru - ly,

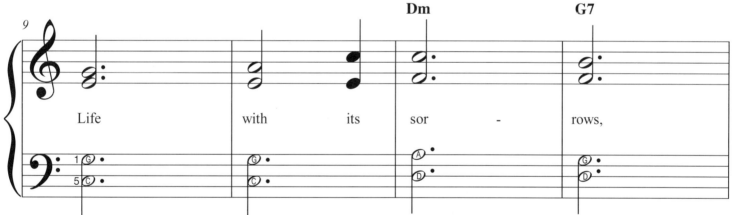

tru - ly, dear.

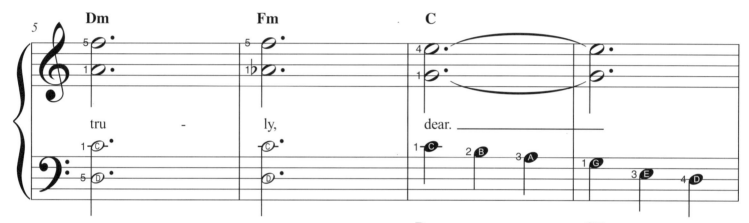

Life with its sor - rows,

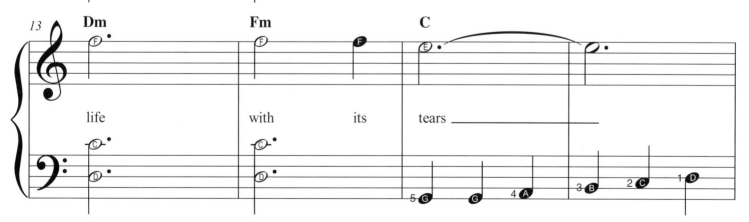

life with its tears

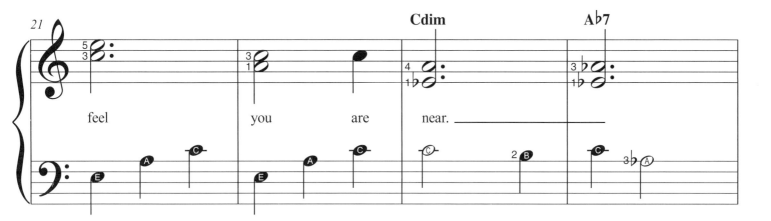

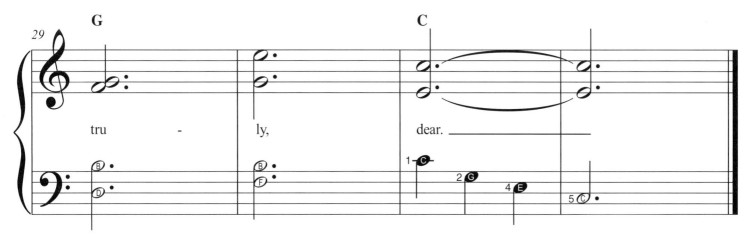

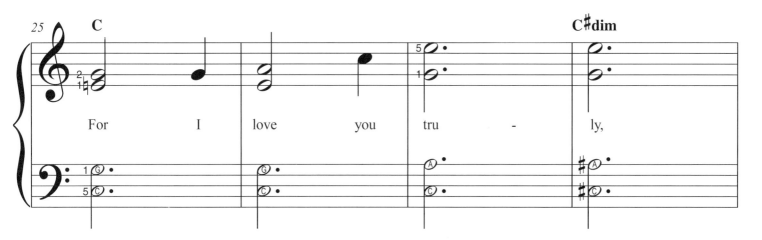

# SKYE BOAT SONG

Words by Robert Louis Stevenson
Traditional Scottish Melody

**Flowing along**

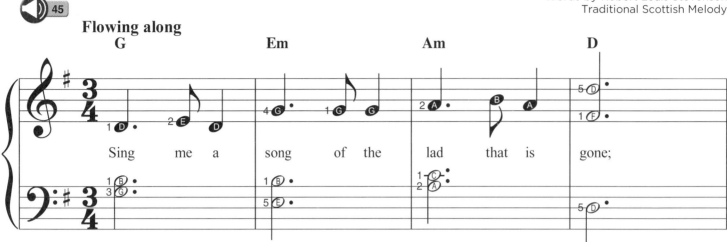

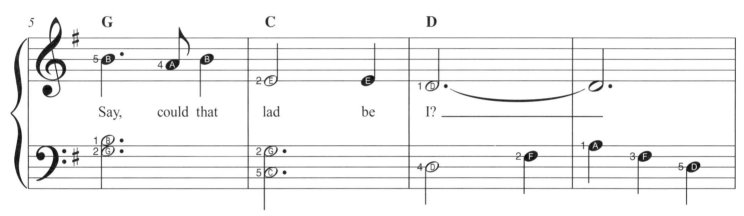

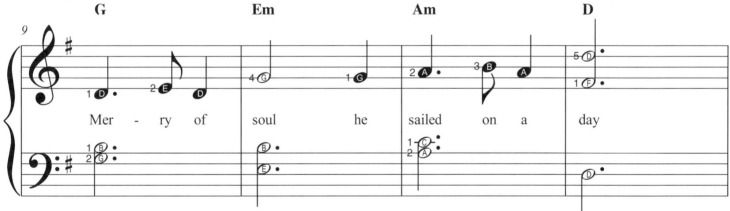

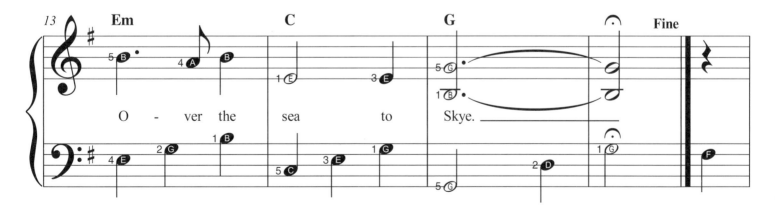

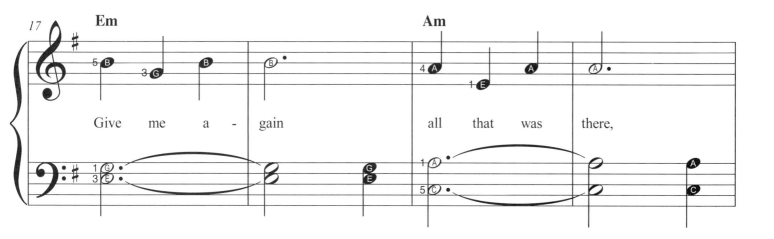

Give me a - gain  all  that  was  there,

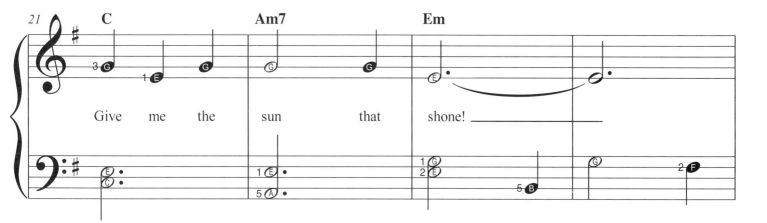

Give  me  the  sun  that  shone! _____

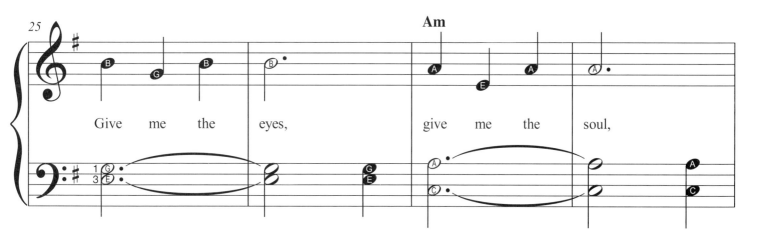

Give  me  the  eyes,  give  me  the  soul,

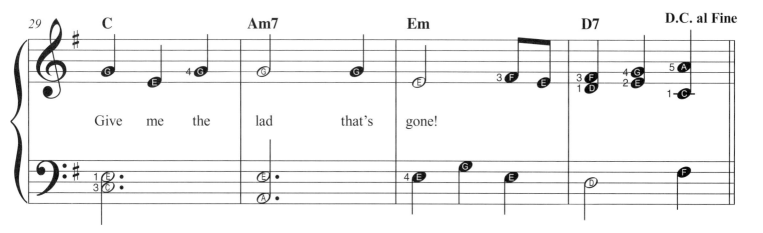

Give  me  the  lad  that's  gone!

**EASY PRO**
**Key: G major**

# SKYE BOAT SONG

Words by Robert Louis Stevenson
Traditional Scottish Melody

46

**Flowing along**

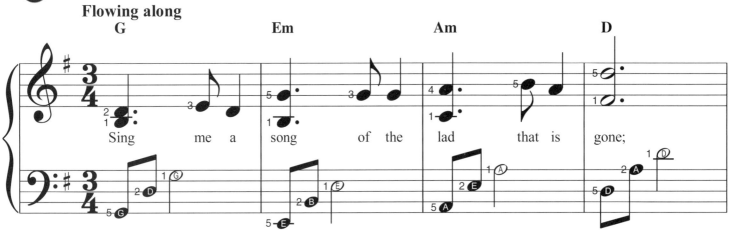

Sing me a song of the lad that is gone;

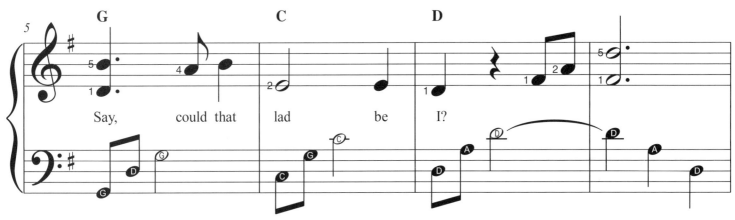

Say, could that lad be I?

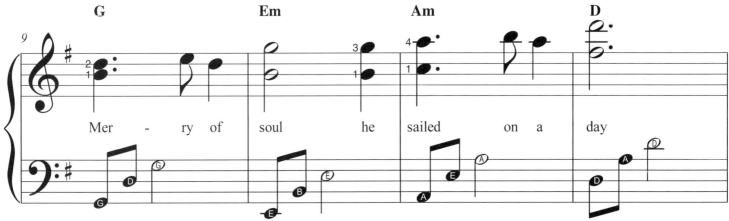

Mer - ry of soul he sailed on a day

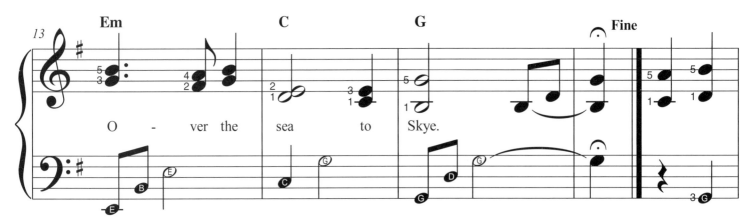

O - ver the sea to Skye.

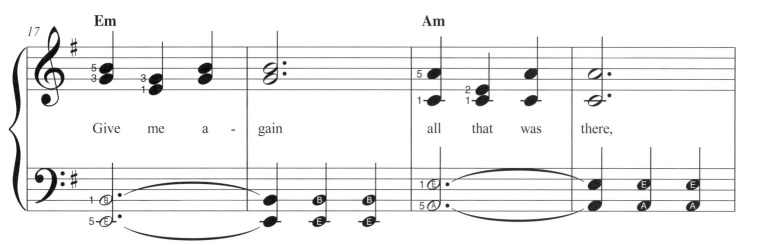

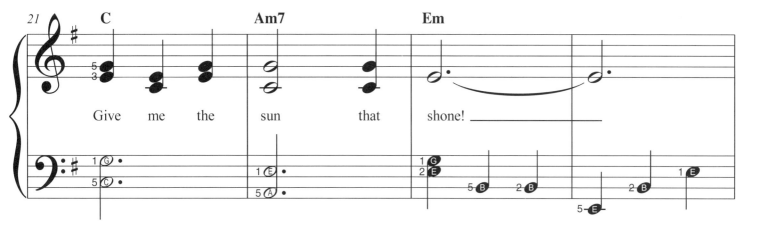

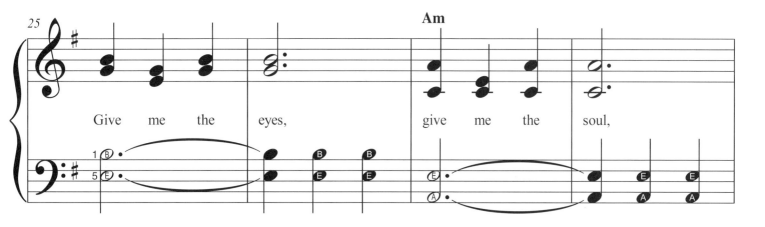

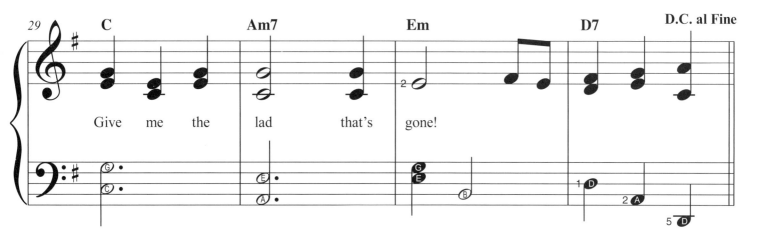

**EASY BEGINNER**
**Key: A minor**

# SCARBOROUGH FAIR

47

Traditional English

**Moderately slow**

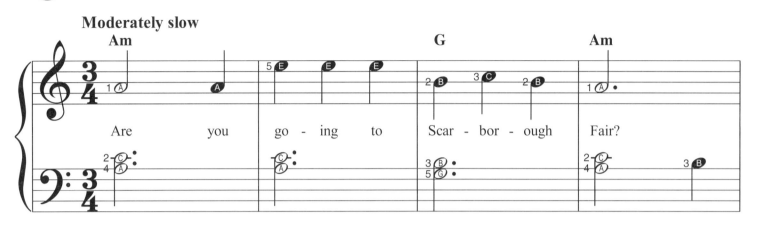

Are you go - ing to Scar - bor - ough Fair?

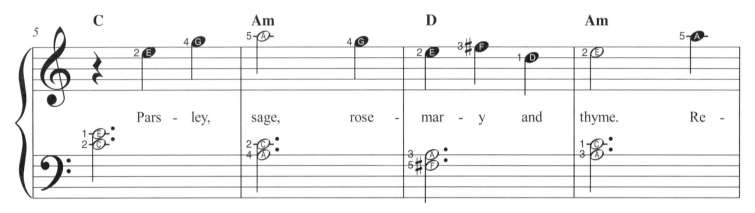

Pars - ley, sage, rose - mar - y and thyme. Re -

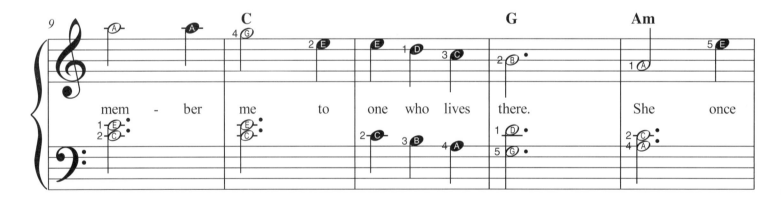

mem - ber me to one who lives there. She once

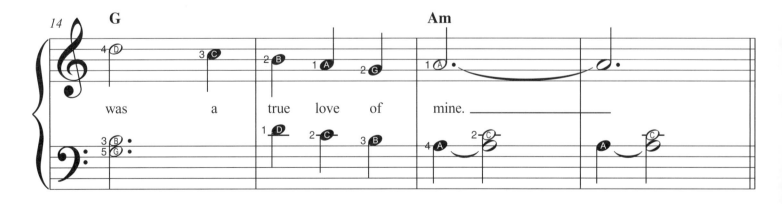

was a true love of mine. _____

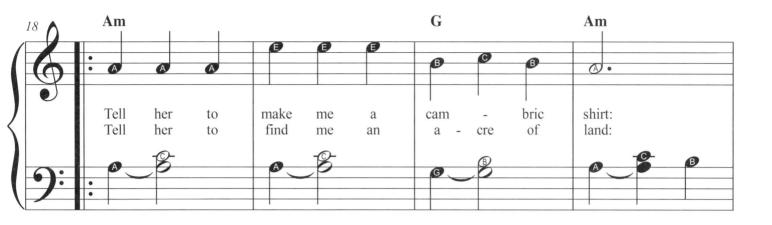

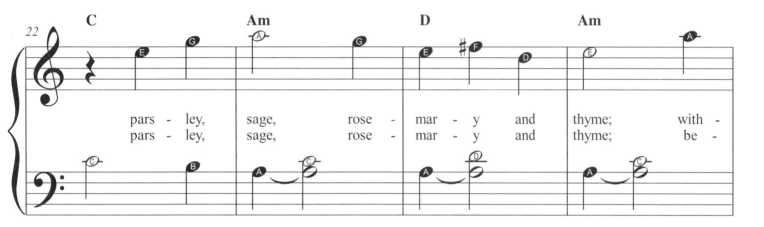

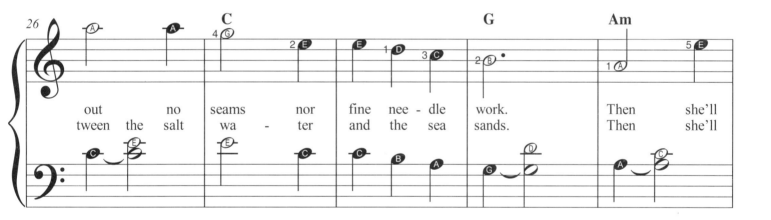

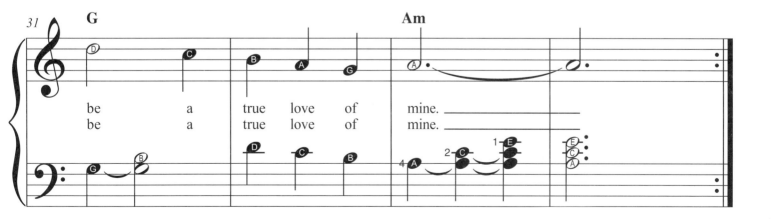

# SCARBOROUGH FAIR

Traditional English

**Moderately slow**

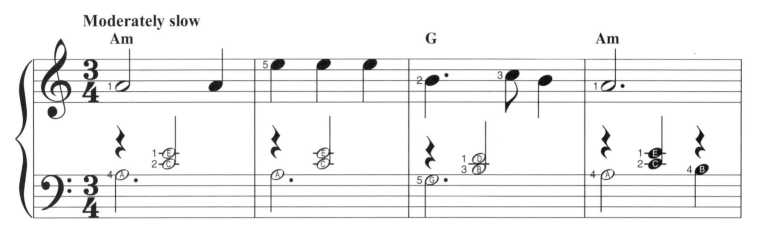

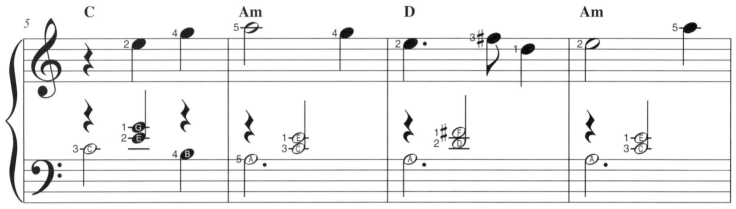

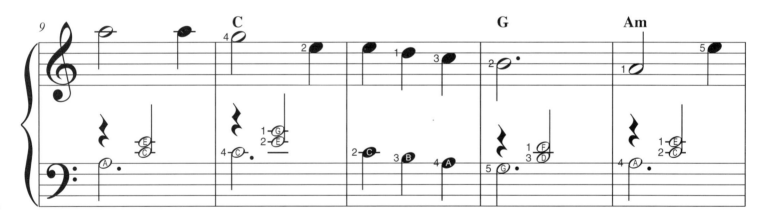

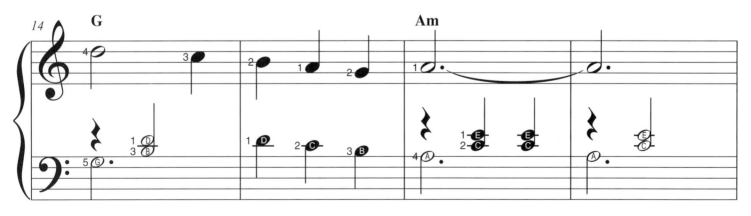

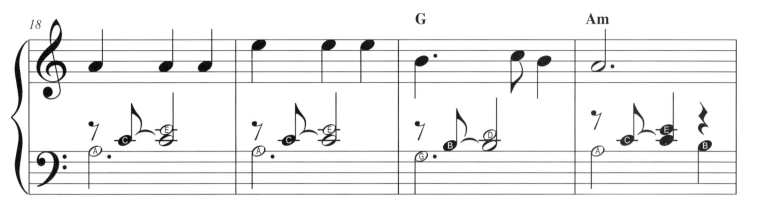

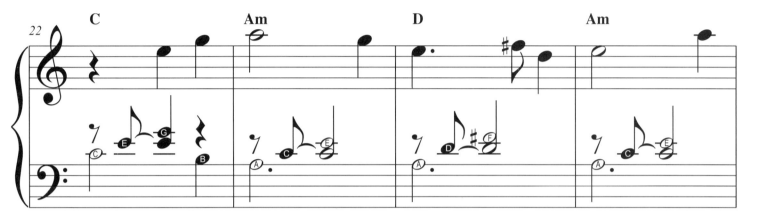

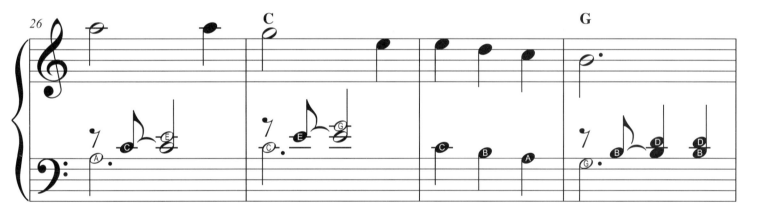

*Arpeggio: Play notes one-at-a-time very quickly from lowest to highest.
The effect is that of strumming a chord on a guitar.

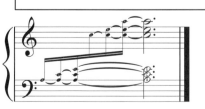

# WHEN THE SAINTS GO MARCHING IN

**EASY PRO**
**Key: C minor**

Words by Katherine E. Purvis
Music by James M. Black

Moderately slow

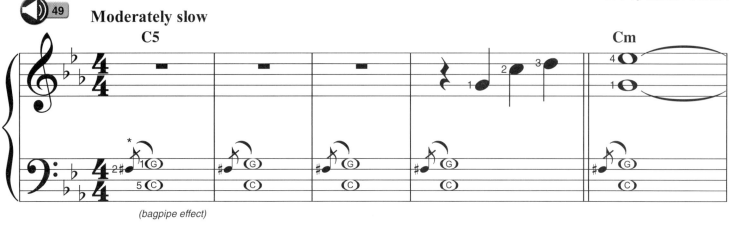

(bagpipe effect)

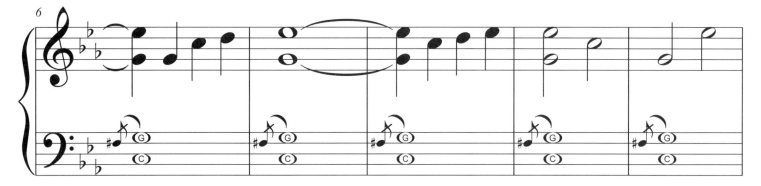

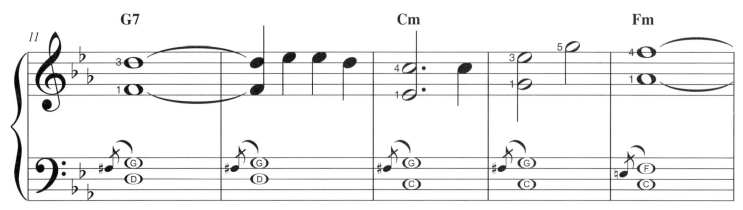

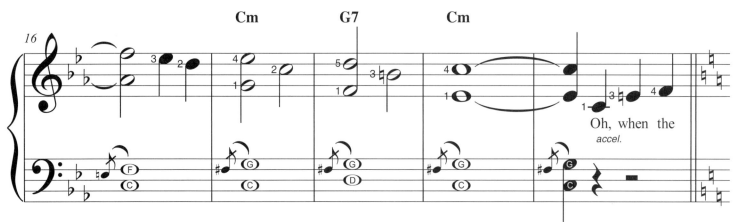

Oh, when the
*accel.*

*Grace notes (optional): Grace notes have no actual time value. They're used to decorate or embellish the note(s) immediately following. Play them as quickly as possible.

**Key: C major**

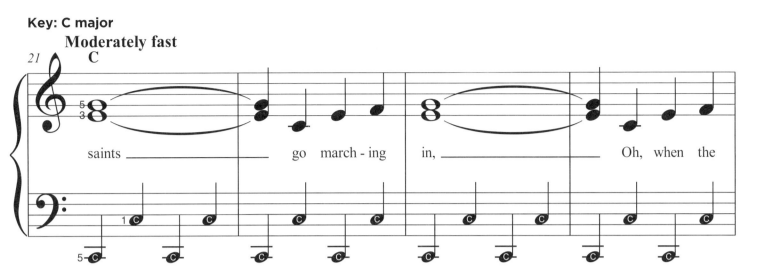

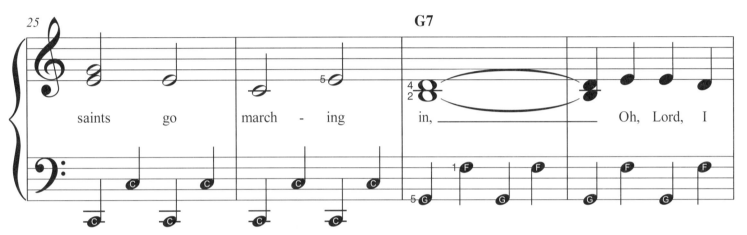

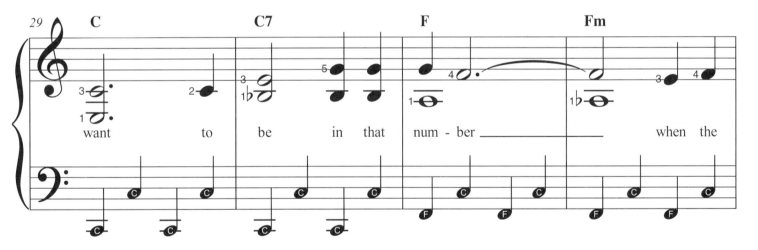

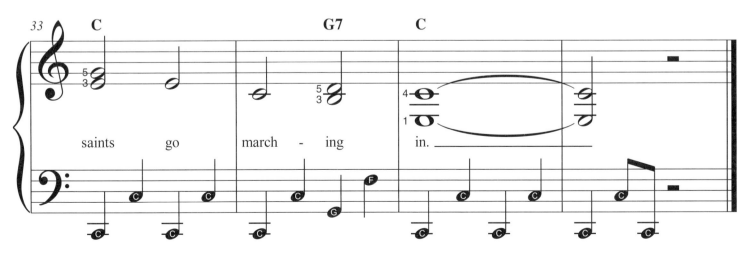

# DANNY BOY
## (Londonderry Air)

Words by Frederick Edward Weatherly
Traditional Irish Folk Melody

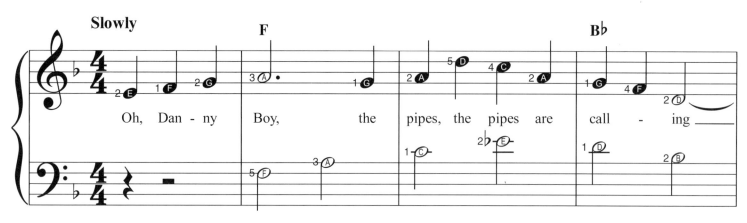

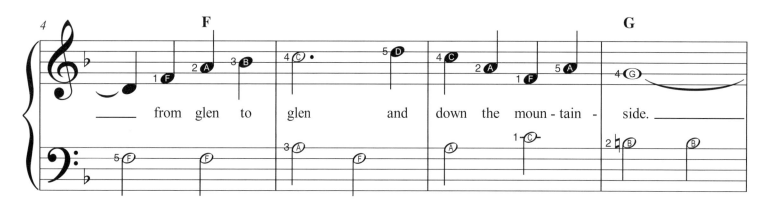

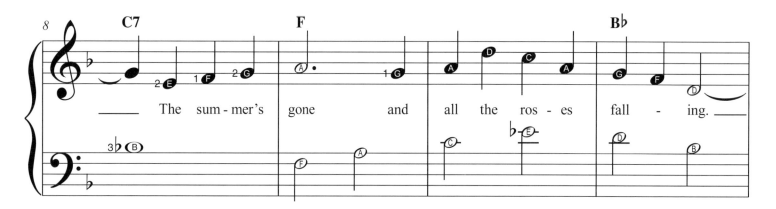

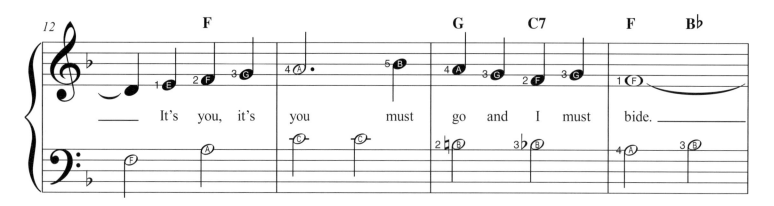

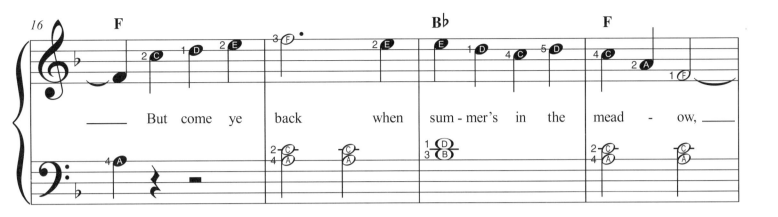

But come ye back when sum - mer's in the mead - ow, _____

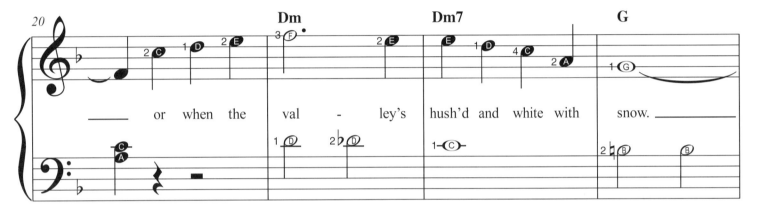

_____ or when the val - ley's hush'd and white with snow. _____

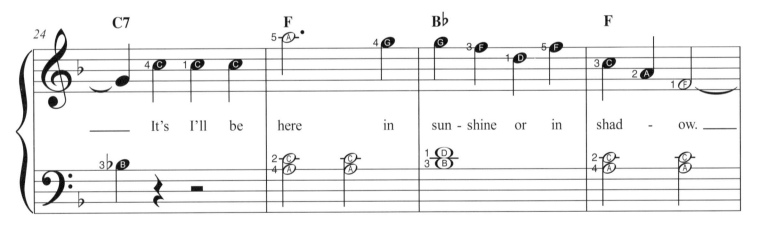

_____ It's I'll be here in sun - shine or in shad - ow.

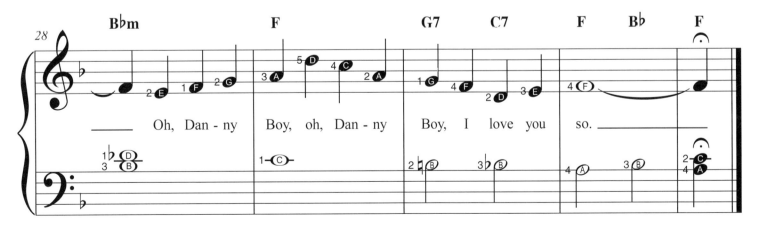

_____ Oh, Dan - ny Boy, oh, Dan - ny Boy, I love you so. _____

# DANNY BOY
## (Londonderry Air)

Words by Frederick Edward Weatherly
Traditional Irish Folk Melody

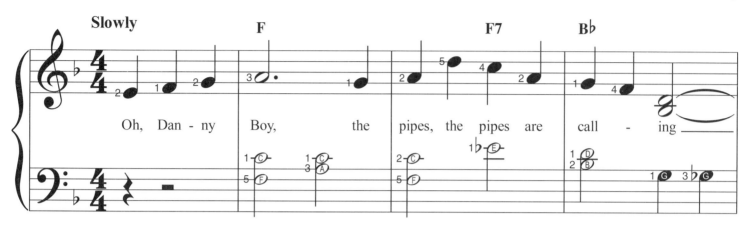

Oh, Dan - ny Boy, the pipes, the pipes are call - ing

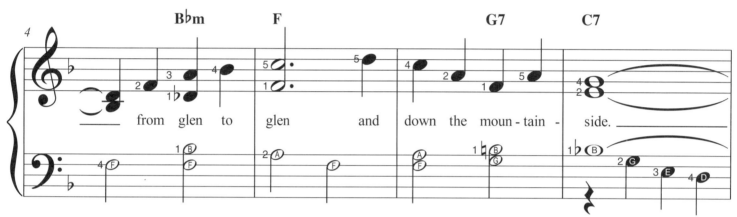

from glen to glen and down the moun - tain - side.

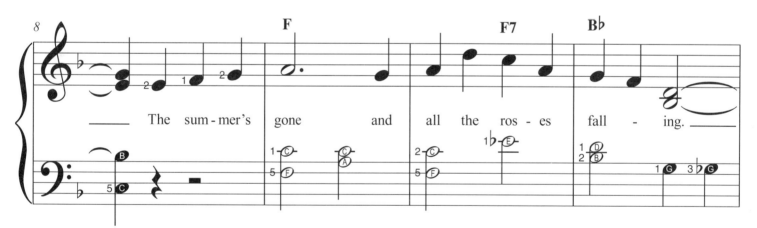

The sum - mer's gone and all the ros - es fall - ing.

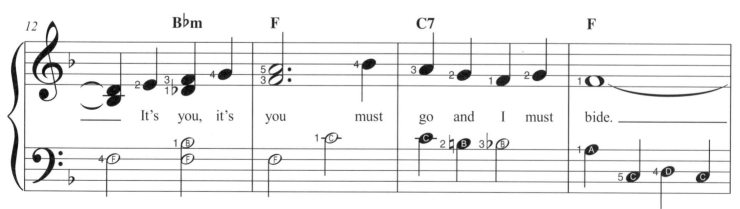

It's you, it's you must go and I must bide.

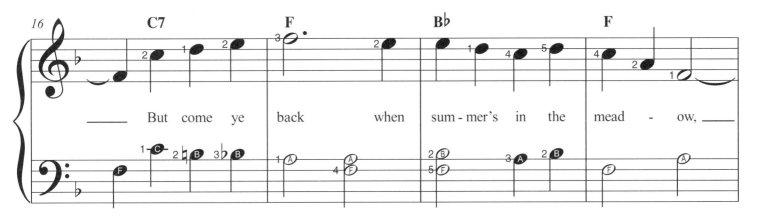

But come ye back when sum-mer's in the mead - ow, ____

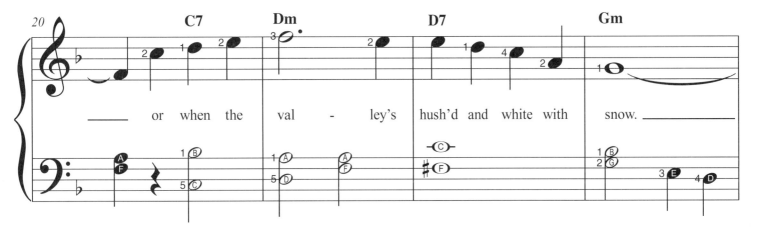

____ or when the val - ley's hush'd and white with snow. ____

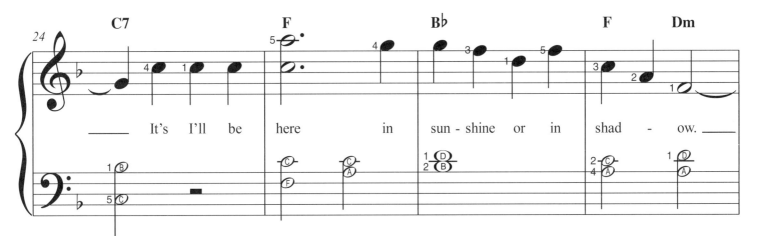

____ It's I'll be here in sun - shine or in shad - ow. ____

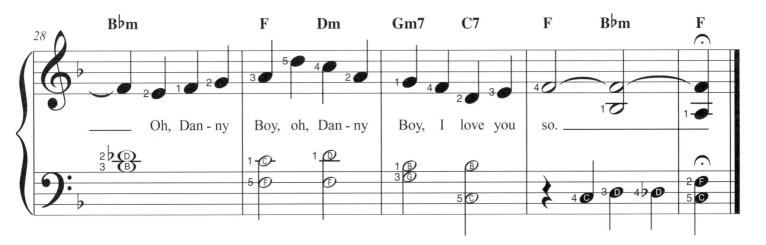

____ Oh, Dan - ny Boy, oh, Dan - ny Boy, I love you so. ____

# GYPSY LOVE SONG

**from THE FORTUNE TELLER**

Words by Harry B. Smith
Music by Victor Herbert

**Moderately; tenderly**

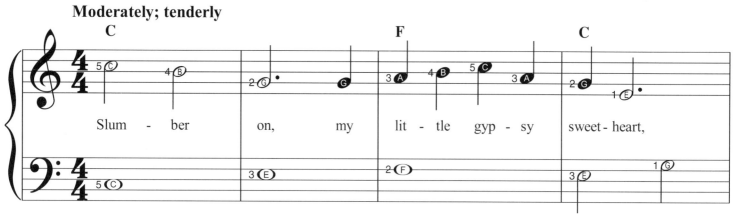

Slum - ber on, my lit - tle gyp - sy sweet - heart,

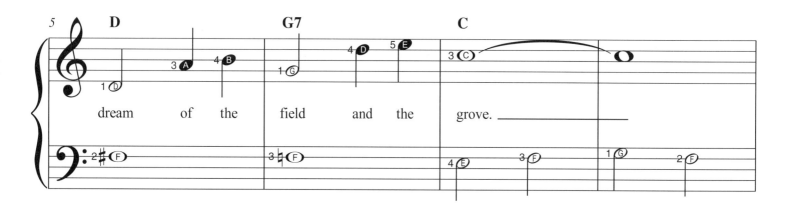

dream of the field and the grove. ____

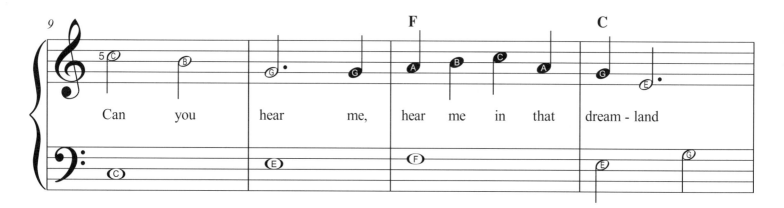

Can you hear me, hear me in that dream - land

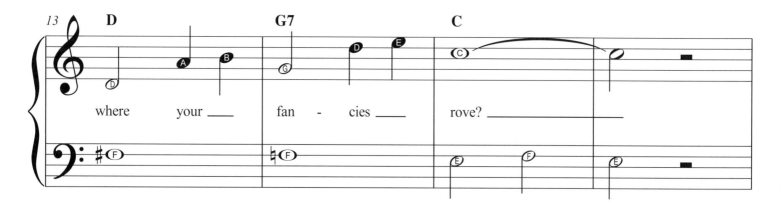

where your ____ fan - cies ____ rove?

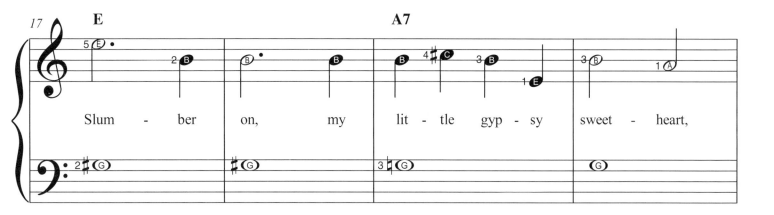

Slum - ber on, my lit - tle gyp - sy sweet - heart,

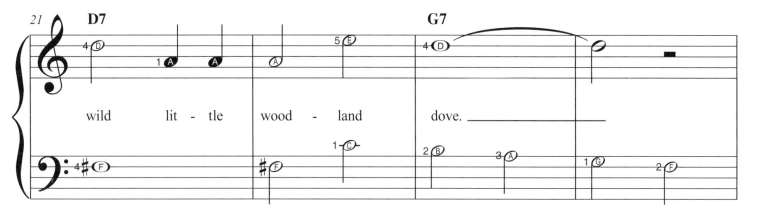

wild lit - tle wood - land dove. _____

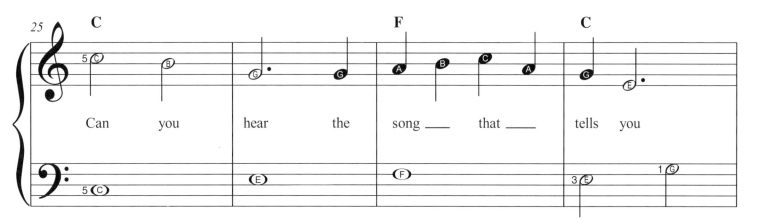

Can you hear the song ___ that ___ tells you

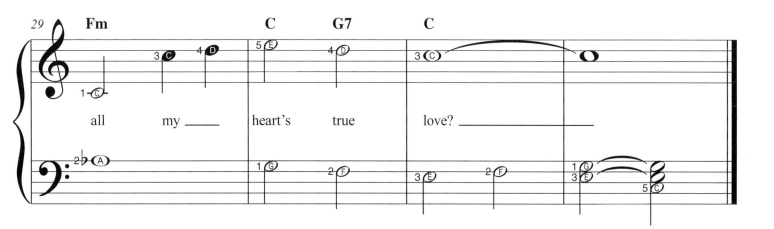

all my ___ heart's true love? _____

# GYPSY LOVE SONG
### from THE FORTUNE TELLER

Words by Harry B. Smith
Music by Victor Herbert

**Moderately; tenderly**

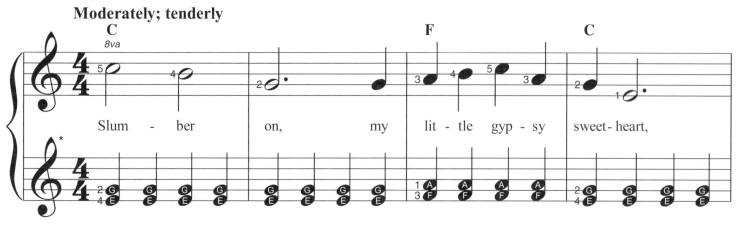

Slum - ber on, my lit - tle gyp - sy sweet - heart,

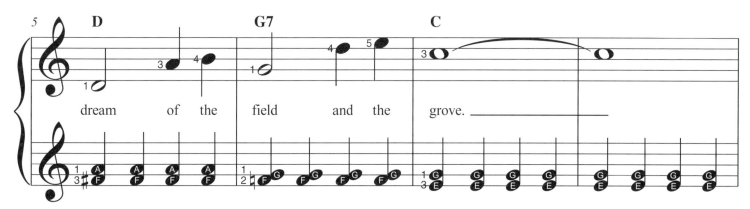

dream of the field and the grove. ___

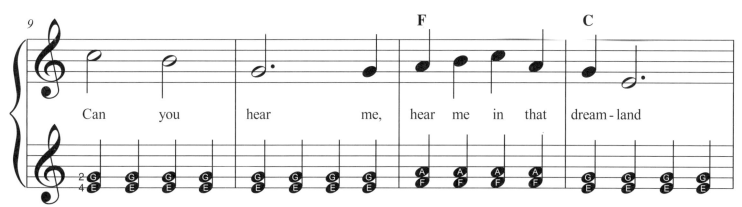

Can you hear me, hear me in that dream - land

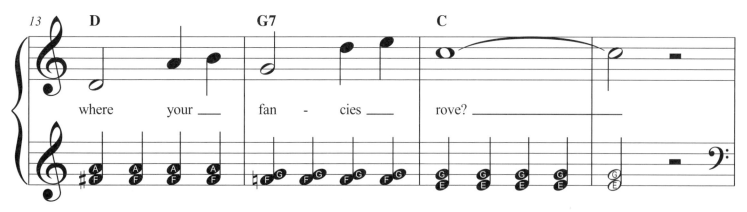

where your ___ fan - cies ___ rove? ___

*Notice that the lower staff is written in TREBLE clef. This is to eliminate the three ledger lines that would be needed if written in bass clef. The bottom staff is still played with the left hand.

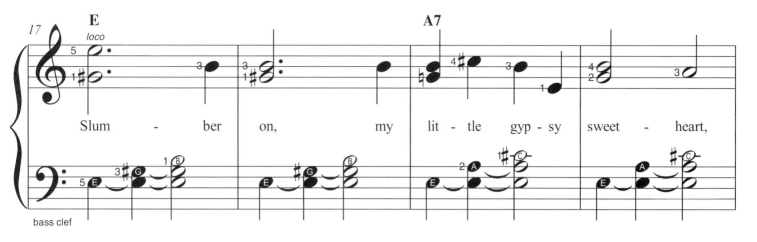

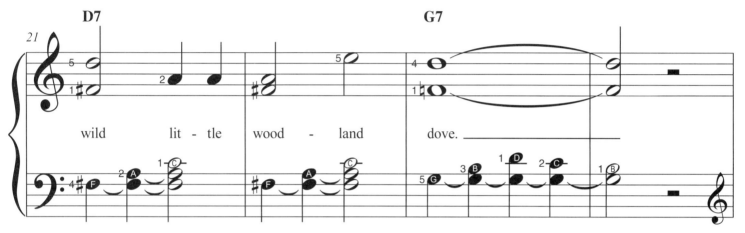

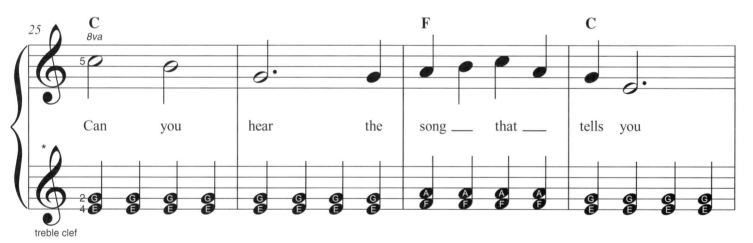

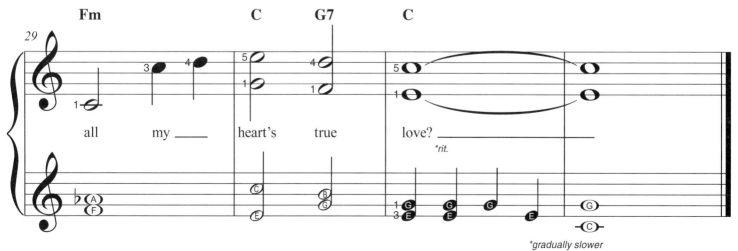

*gradually slower

137

**EASY BEGINNER**
**Key: C Major**

# FASCINATION
### (Valse Tzigane)

By F.D. Marchetti

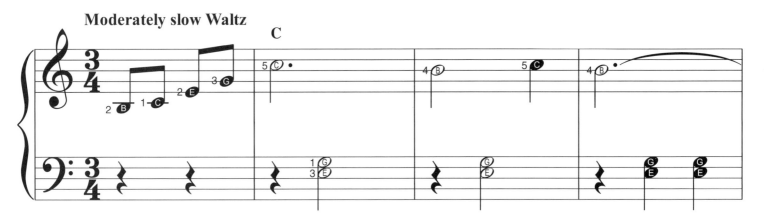

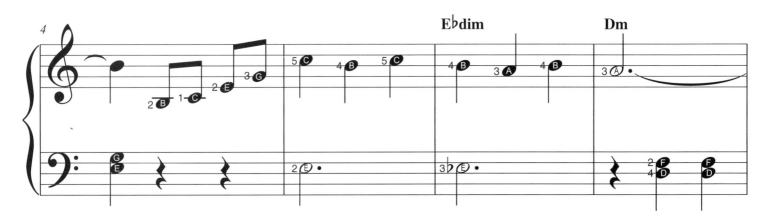

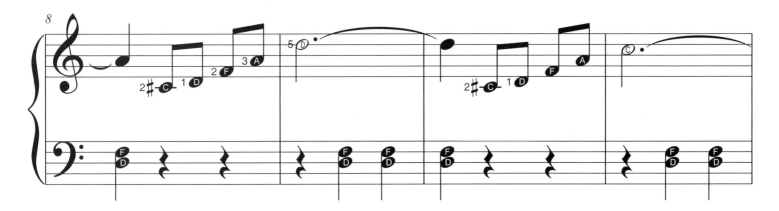

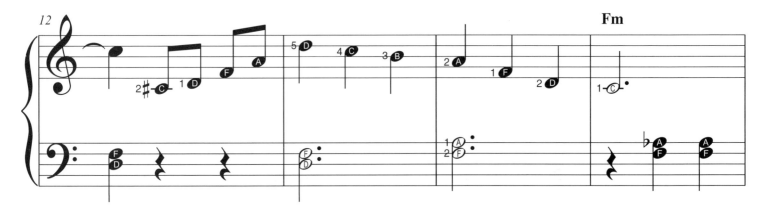

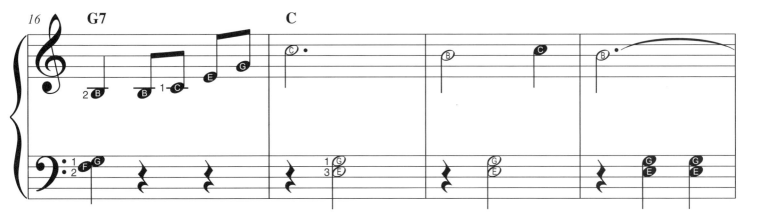

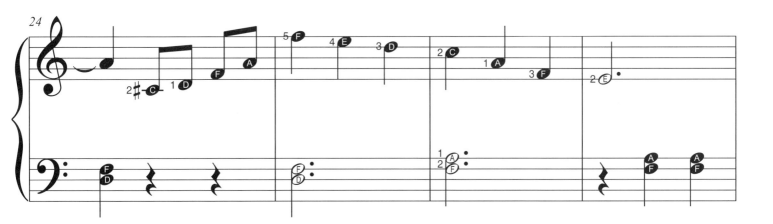

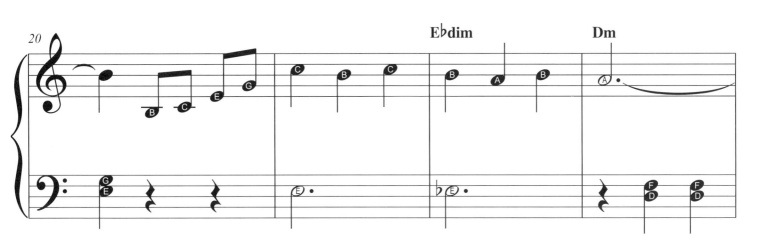

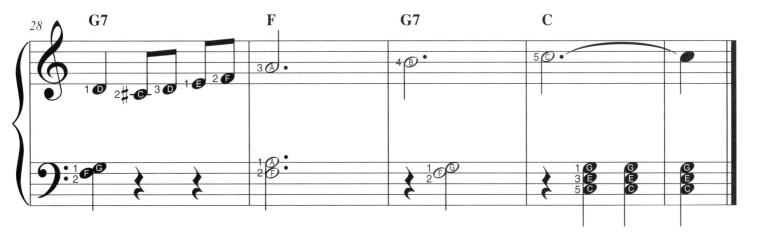

# FASCINATION
### (Valse Tzigane)

By F.D. Marchetti

**Moderately slow Waltz**

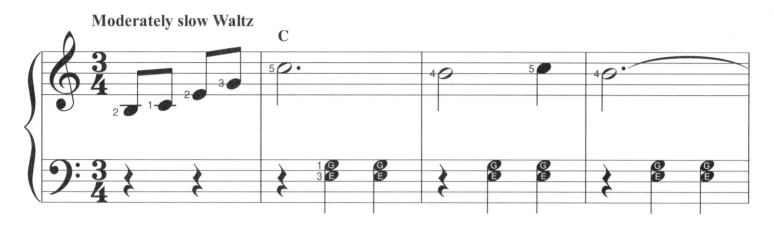

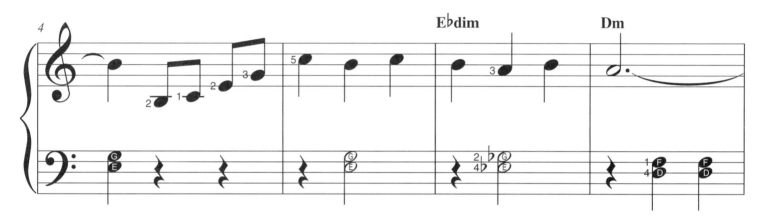

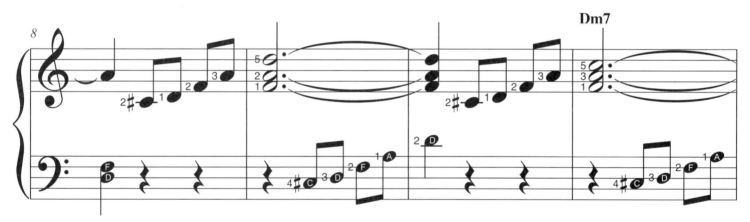

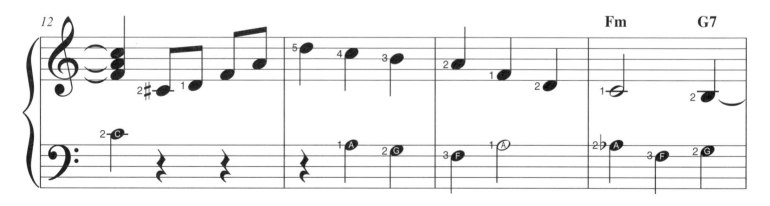

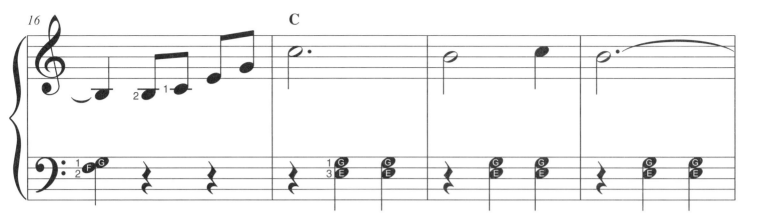

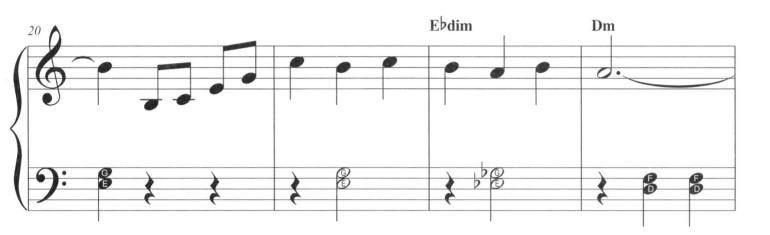

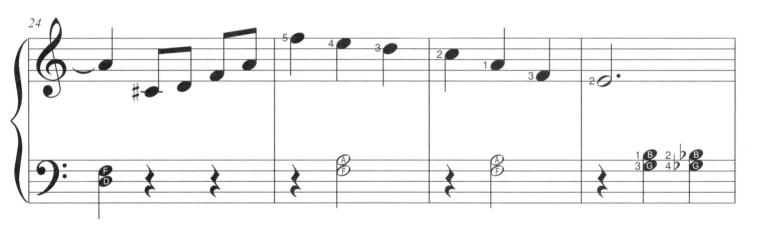

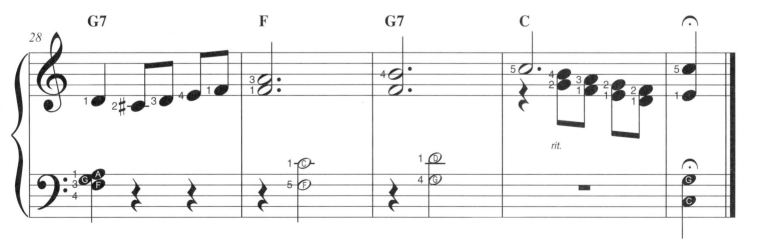

# TO A WILD ROSE
## from WOODLAND SKETCHES

By Edward MacDowell
Op. 51, No. 1

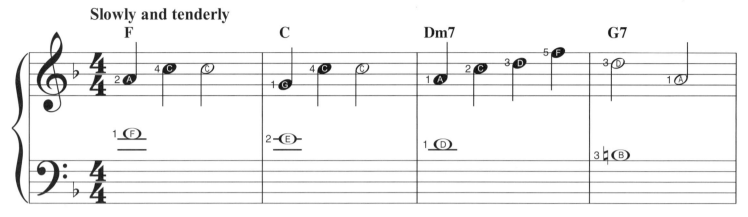

**Slowly and tenderly**

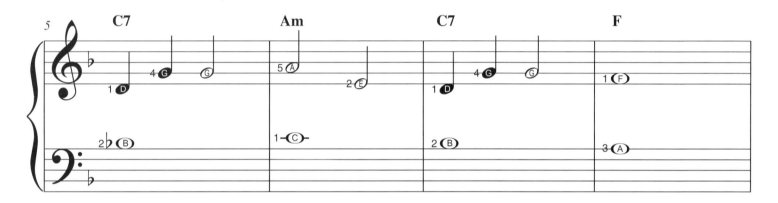

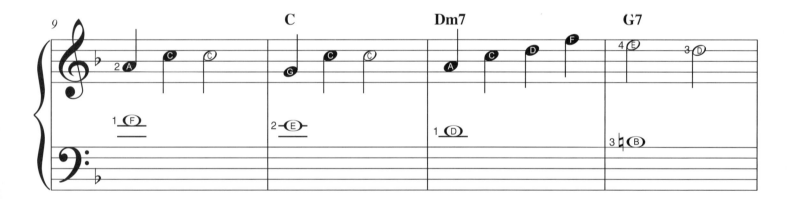

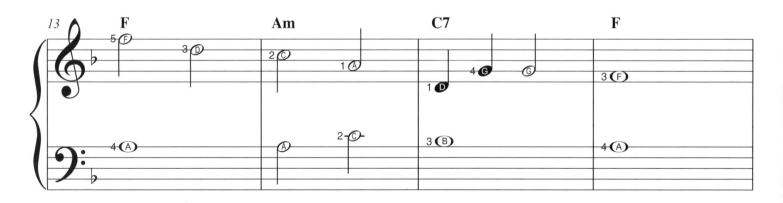

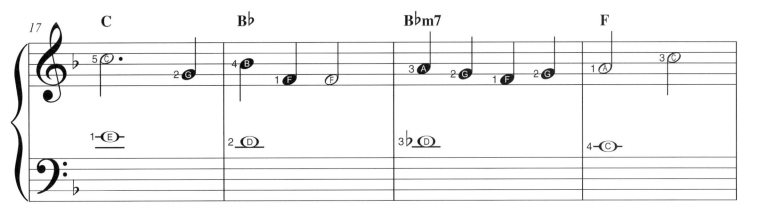

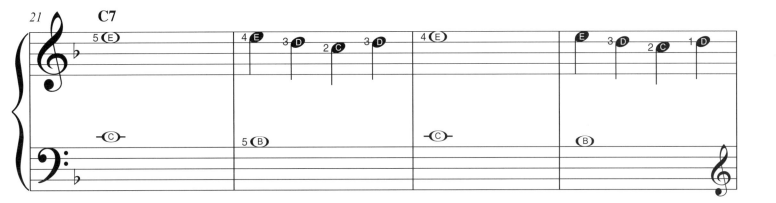

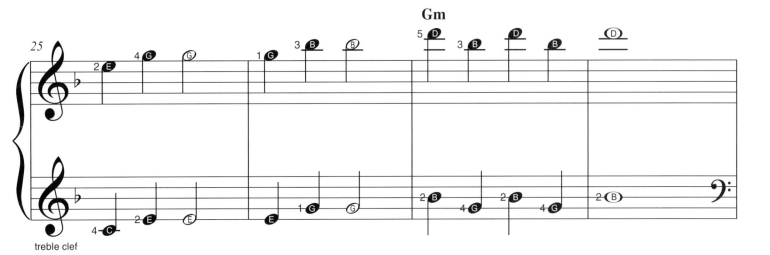

treble clef

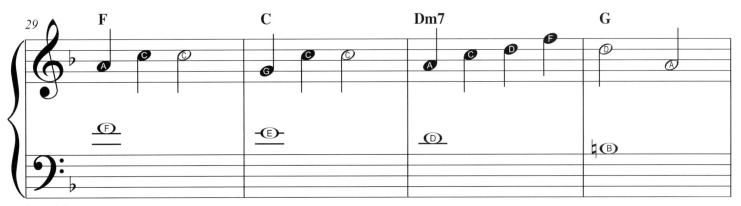

bass clef

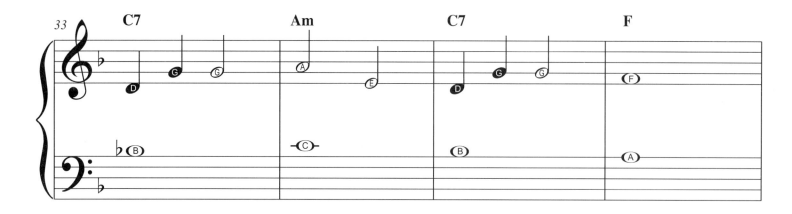

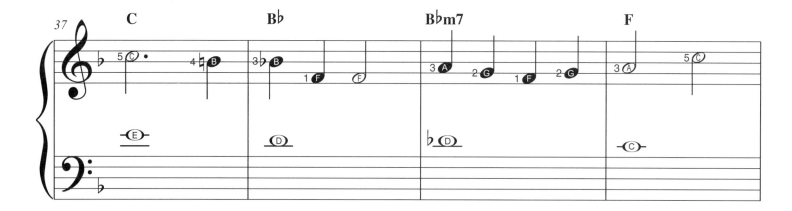

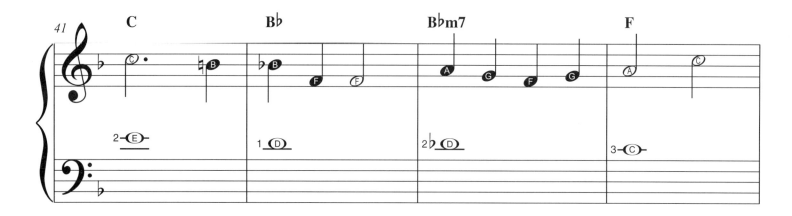

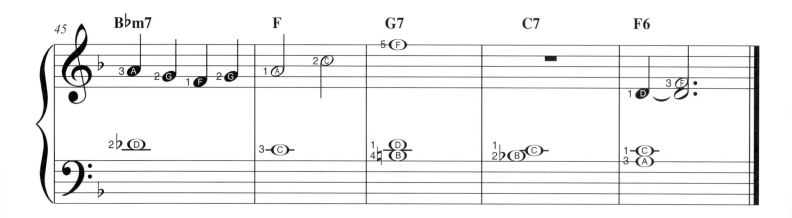

# TO A WILD ROSE

**from WOODLAND SKETCHES**

By Edward MacDowell
Op. 51, No. 1

**Slowly and tenderly**

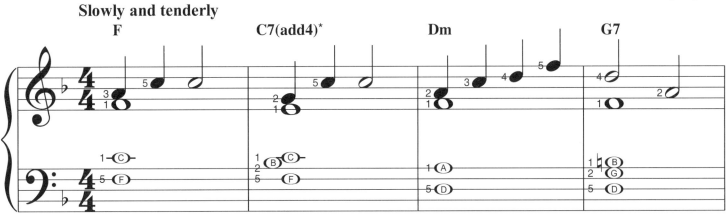

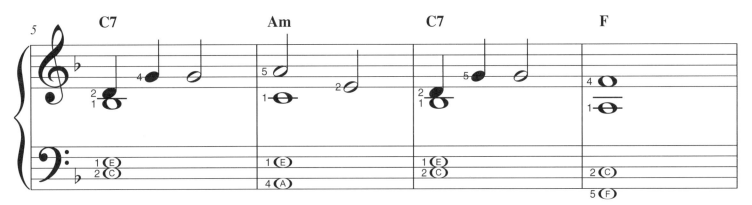

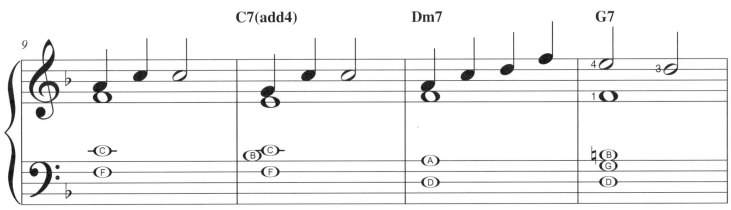

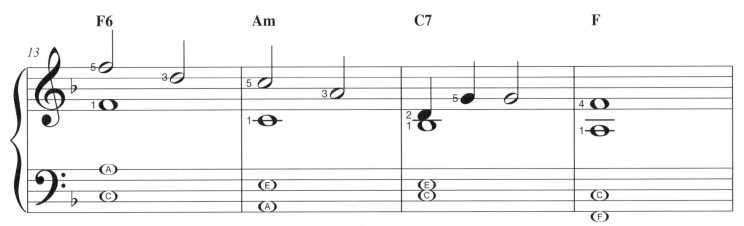

*The (add4) indicates the addition of the 4th note of the C scale; in this case, F.

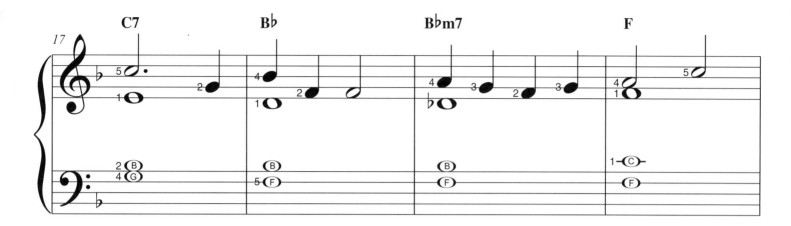

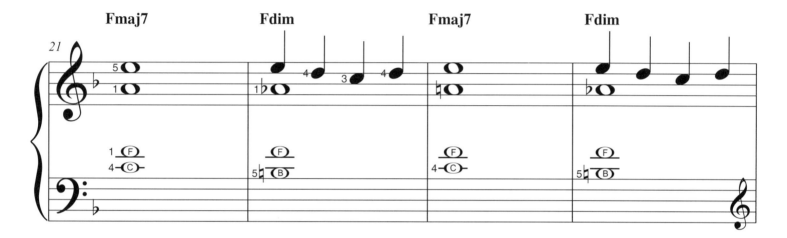

treble clef

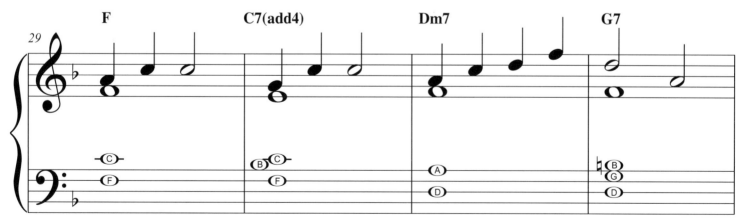

bass clef

146

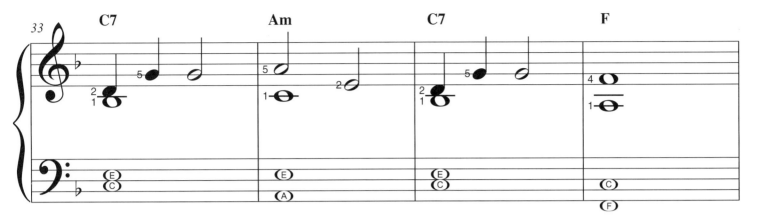

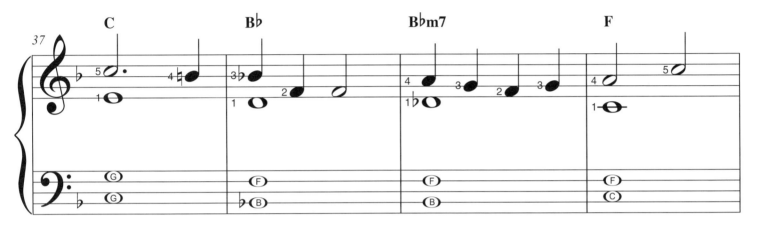

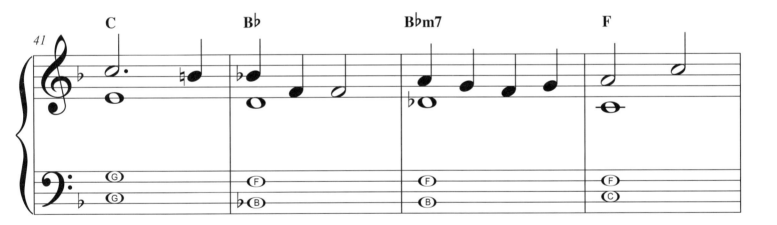

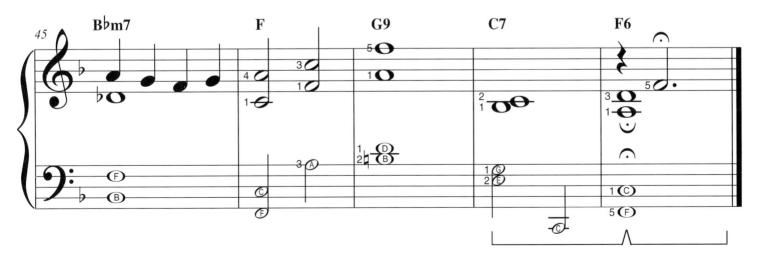

# CAN CAN
## from ORPHEUS IN THE UNDERWORLD

By Jacques Offenbach

**Moderately fast**

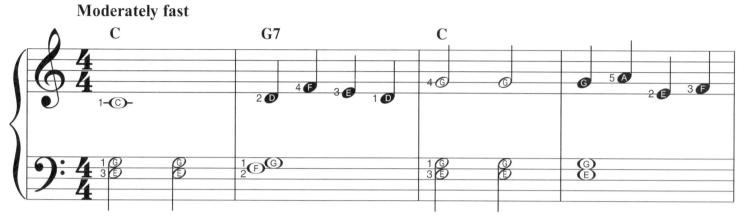

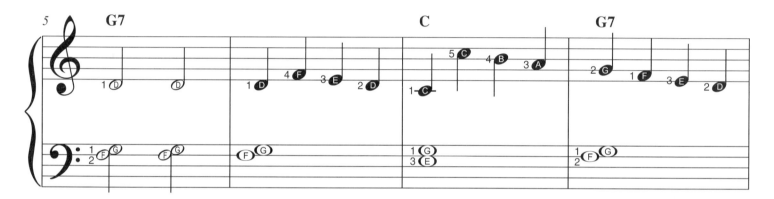

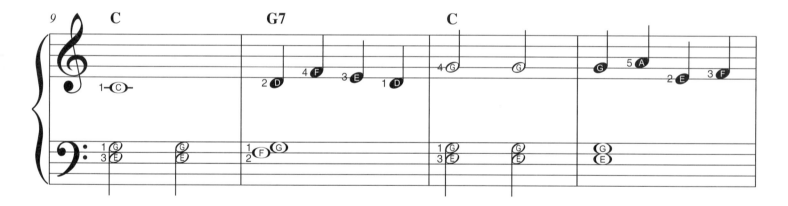

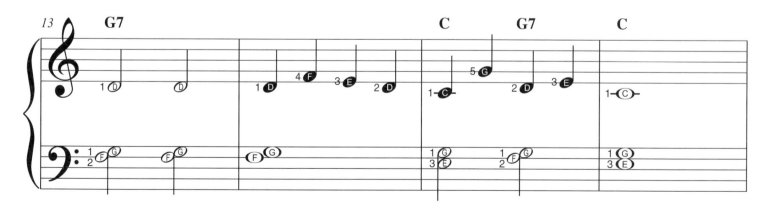

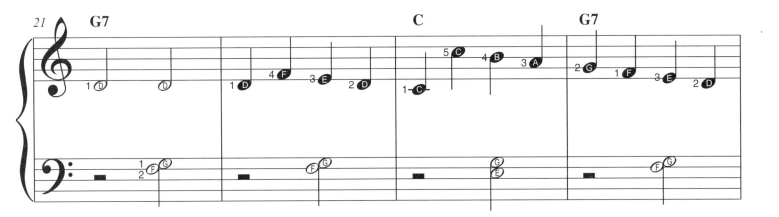

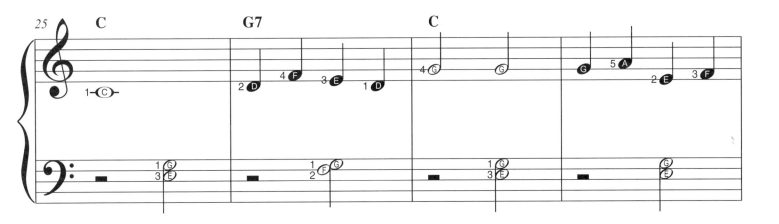

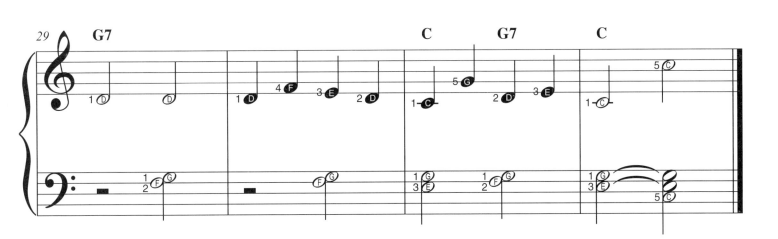

**EASY PRO**
**Key: C major**

# CAN CAN
## from ORPHEUS IN THE UNDERWORLD

By Jacques Offenbach

**Moderately fast**

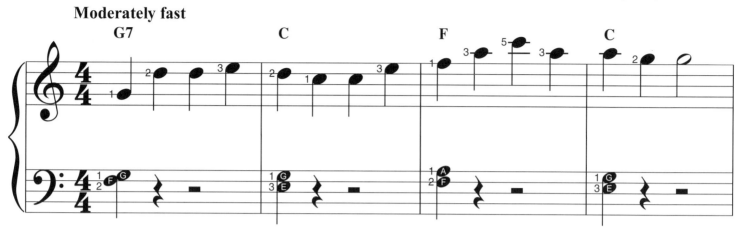

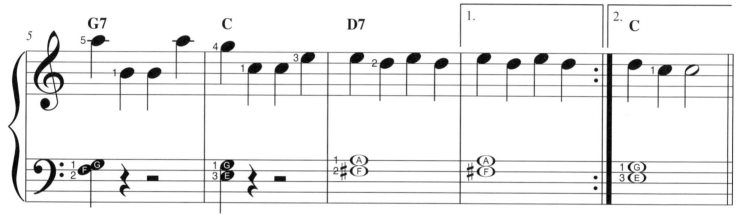

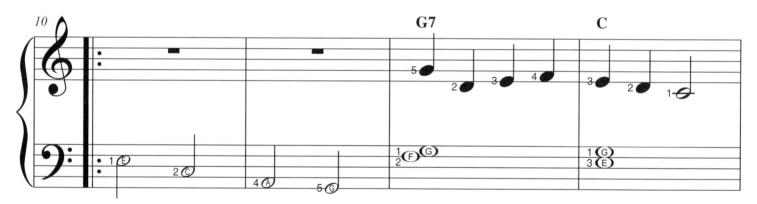

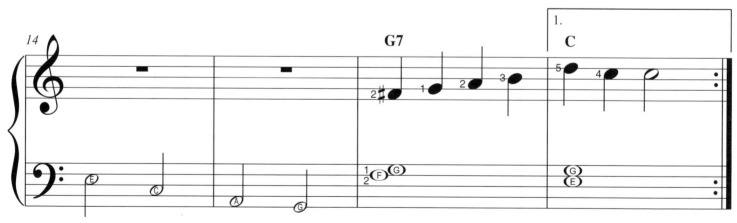

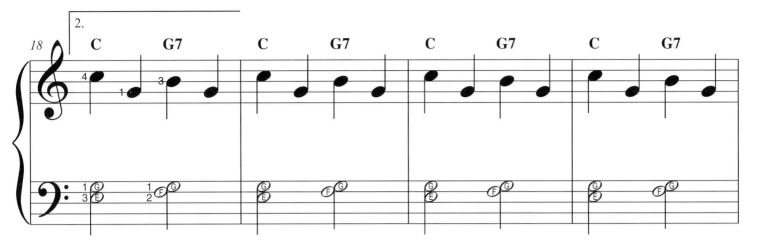

**Key: F major**

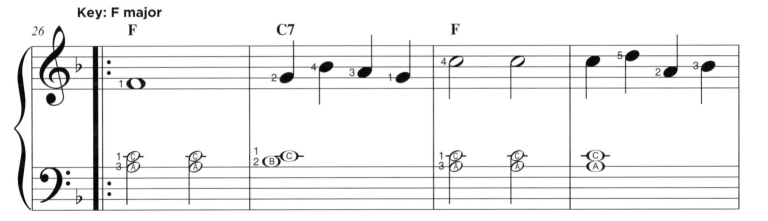

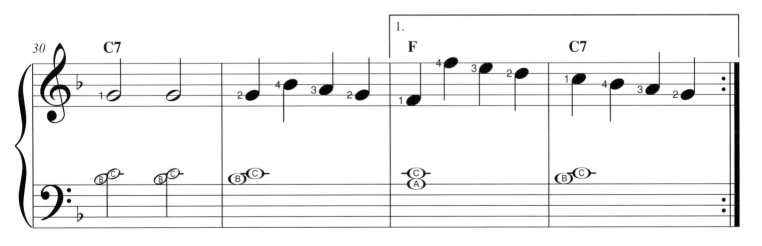

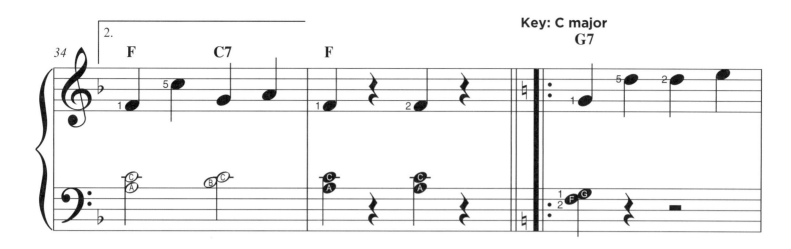

**Key: C major**

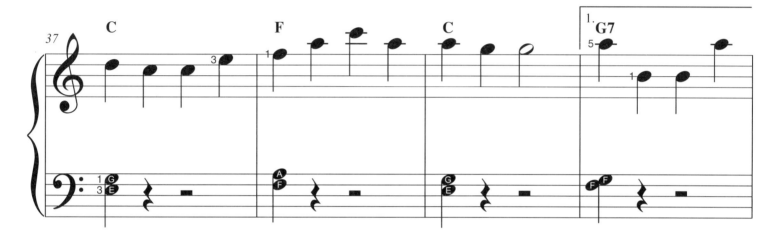

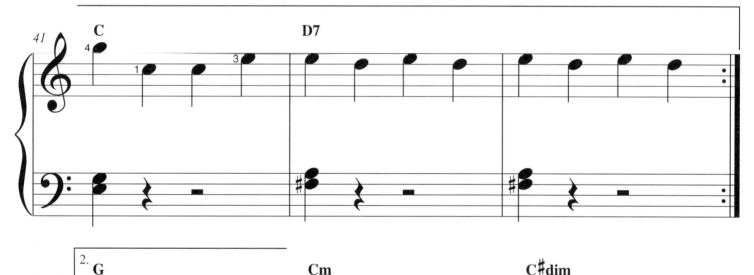

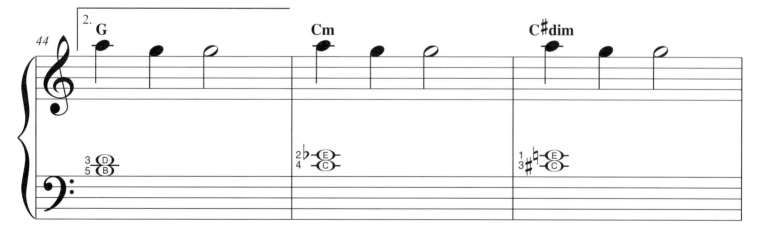

152

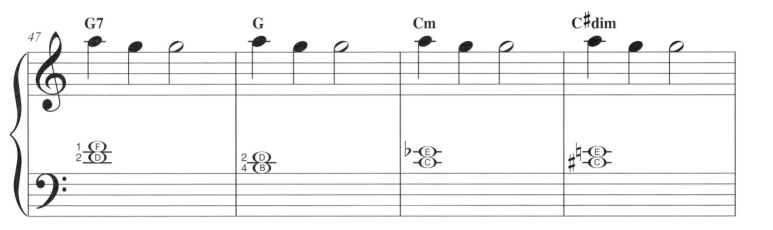

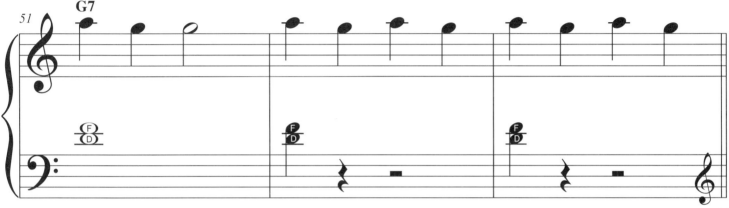

treble clef

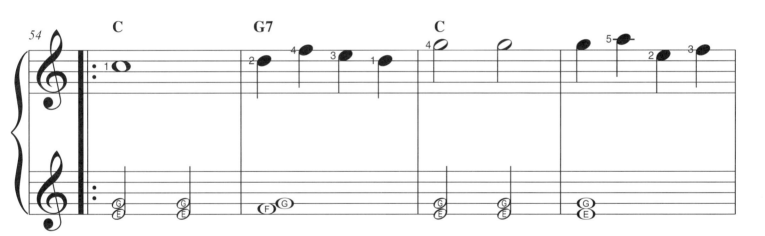

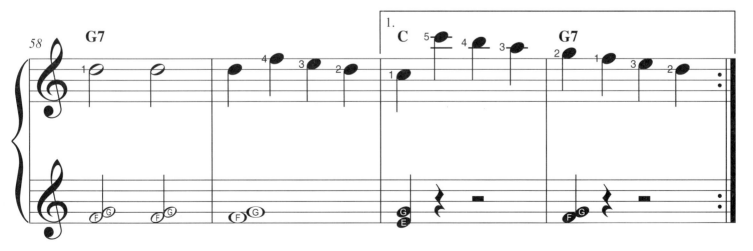

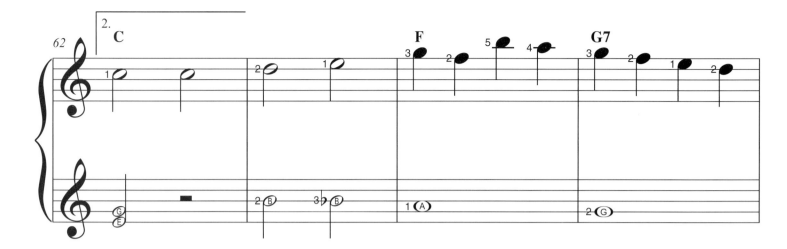

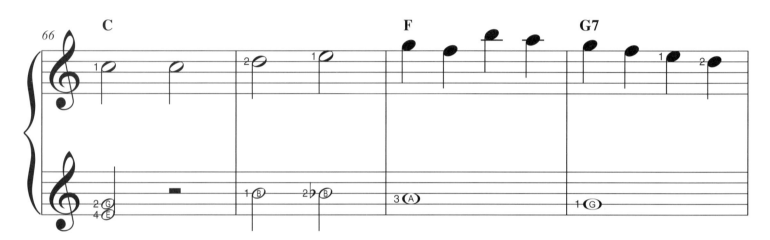

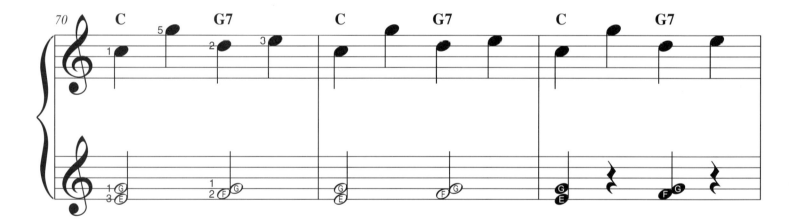

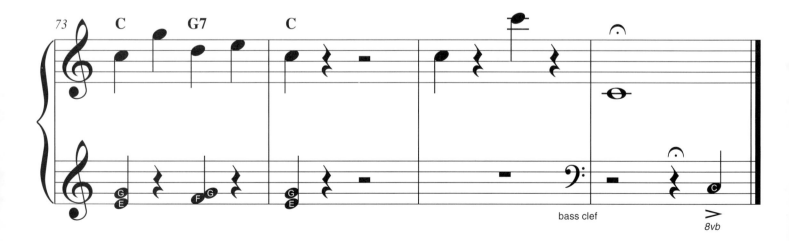

# THE SKATERS
### (Waltz)

By Emil Waldteufel

**Moderately fast Waltz**

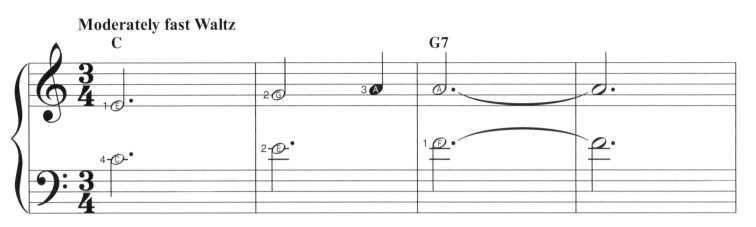

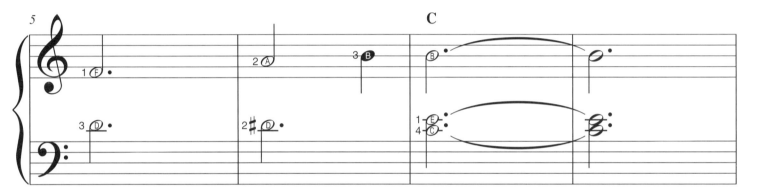

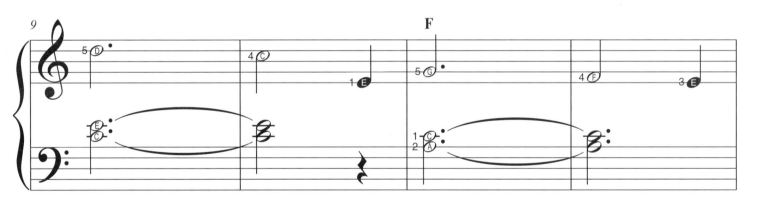

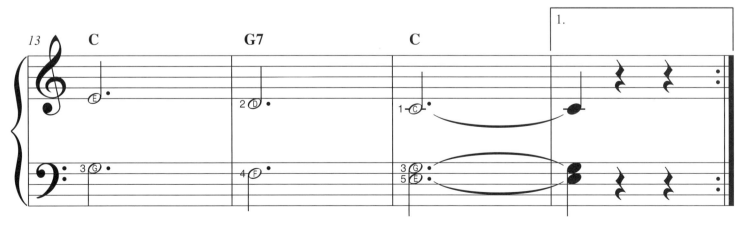

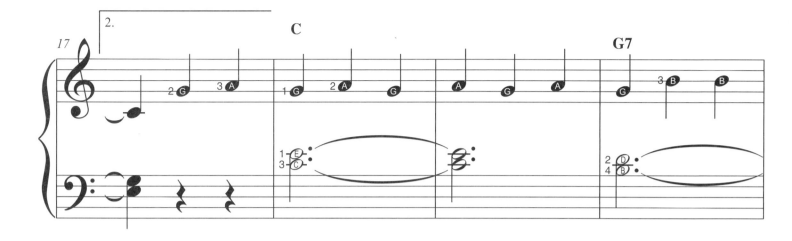

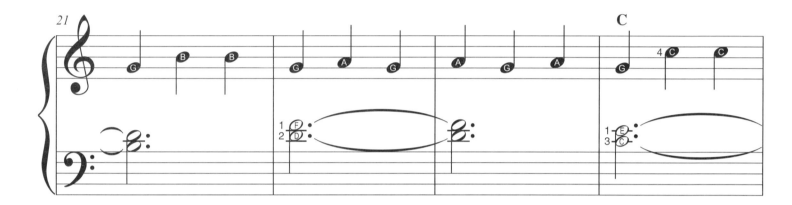

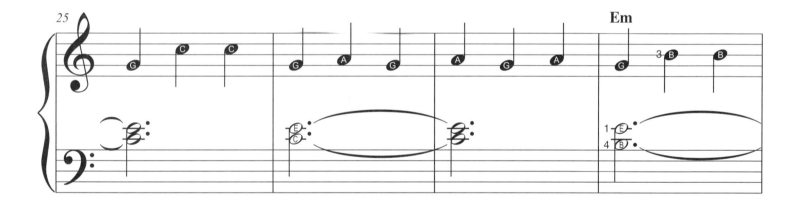

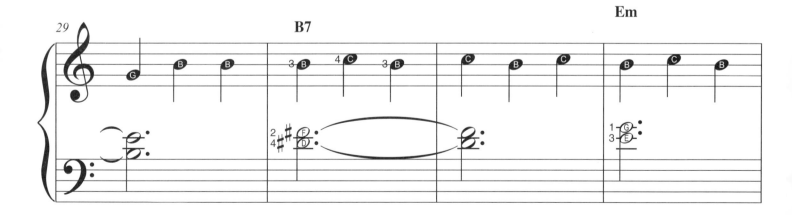

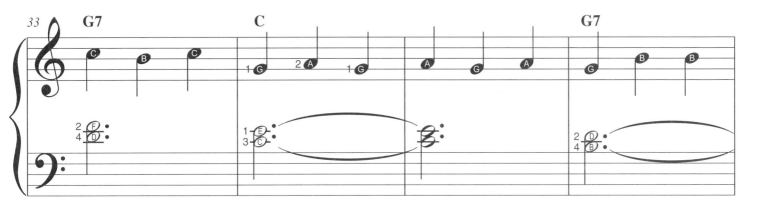

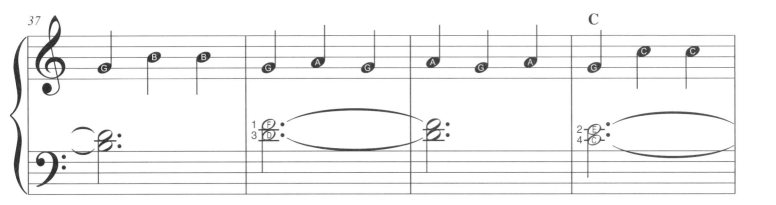

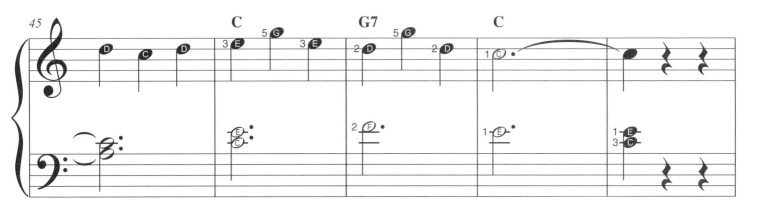

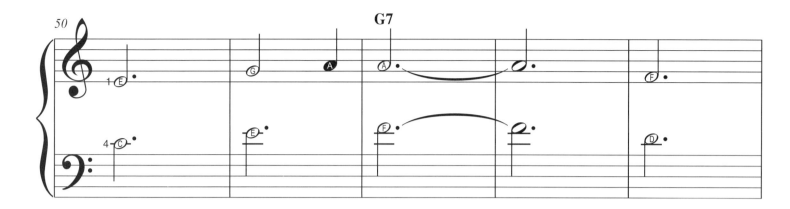

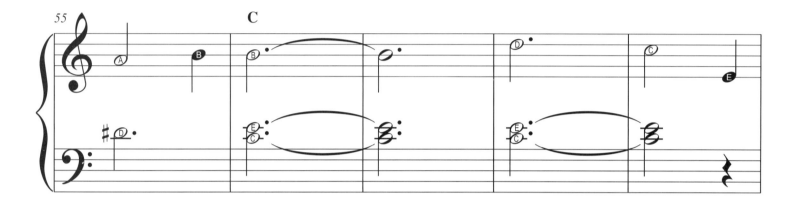

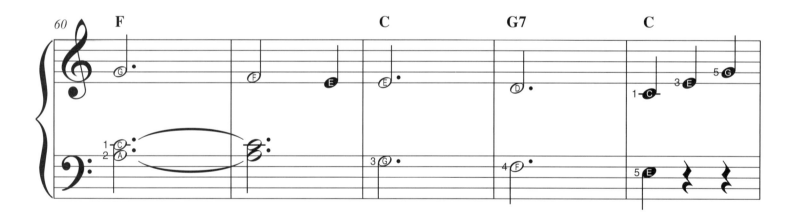

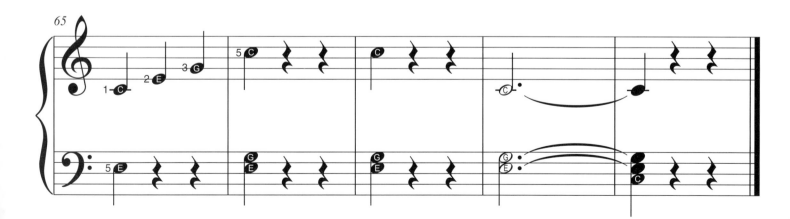

# THE SKATERS
### (Waltz)

By Emil Waldteufel

**Moderately fast Waltz**

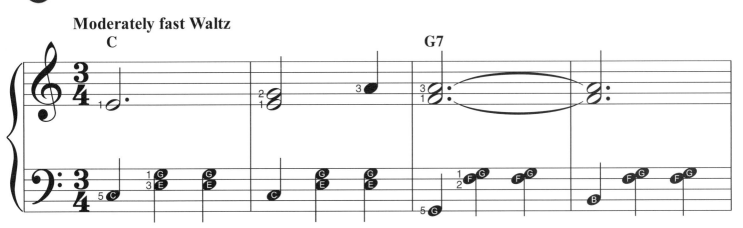

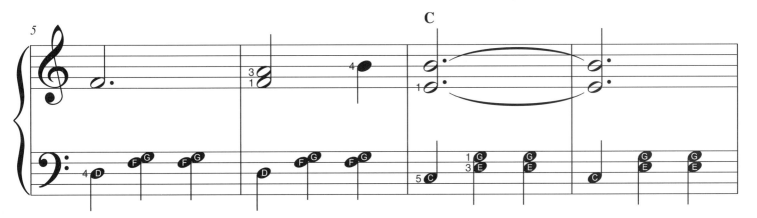

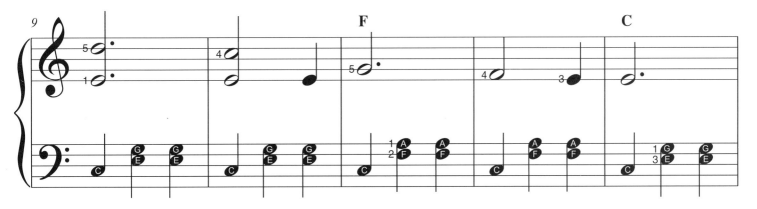

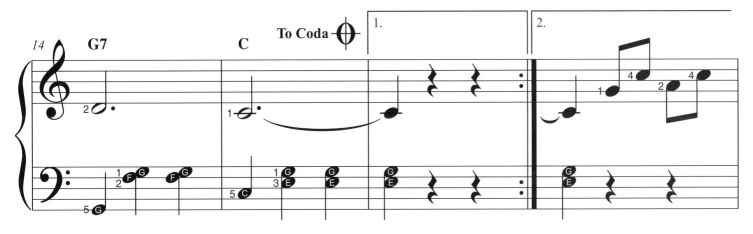

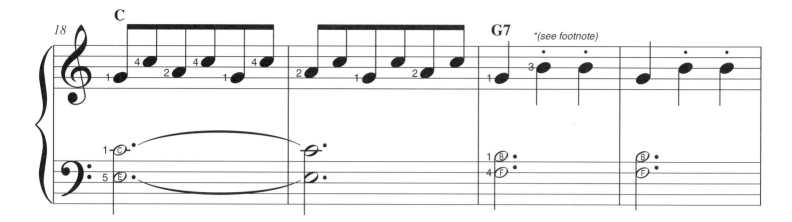

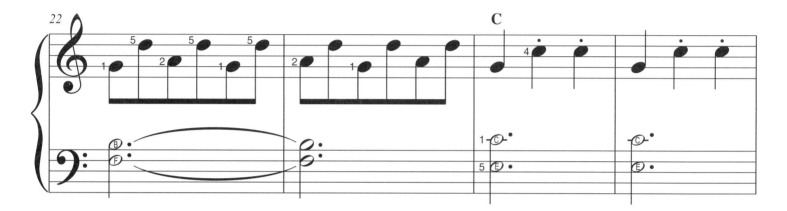

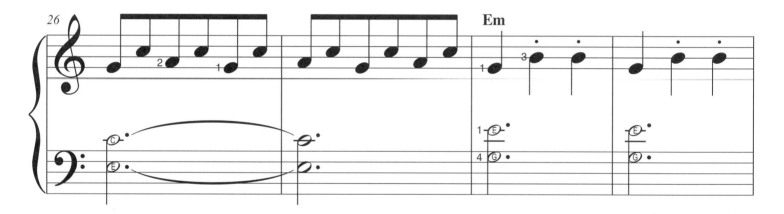

*A dot placed above or below a note (not to the side, as with a dotted-half note 𝅘𝅥𝅭), indicates staccato.
The note is played very short: strike and release the key instantly. The results can be compared to
playing eighth notes followed by eighth rests:

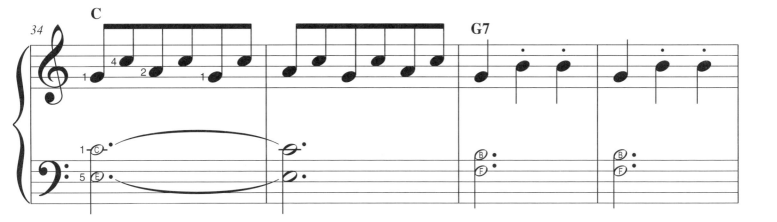

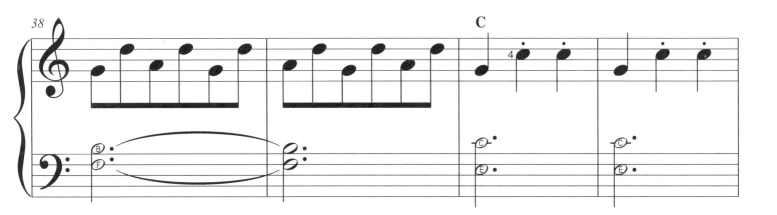

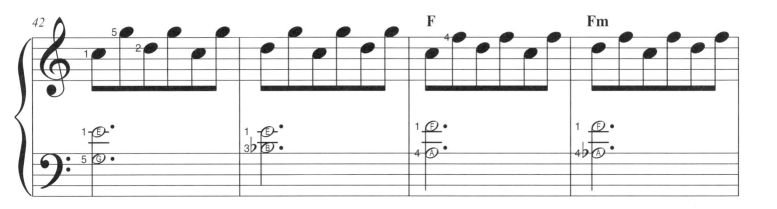

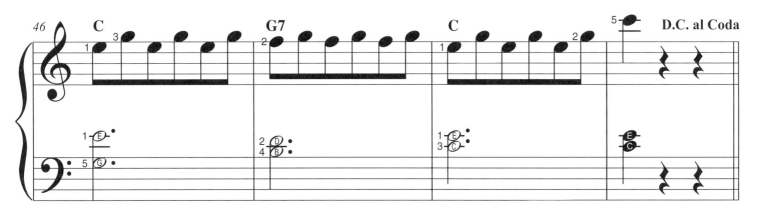

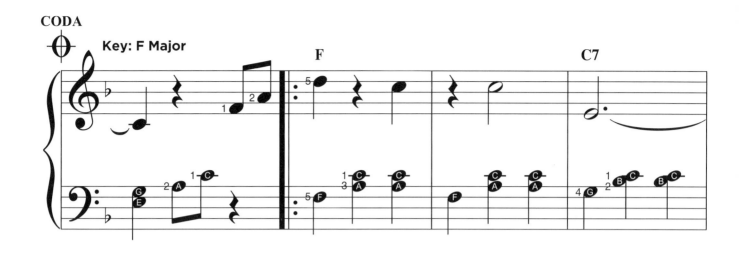

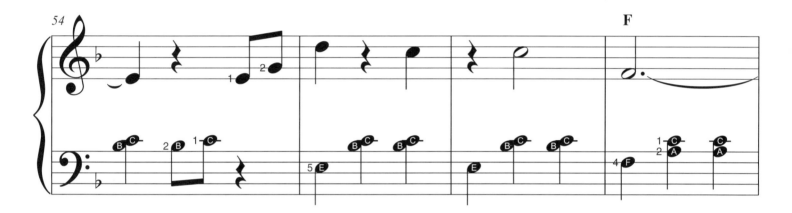

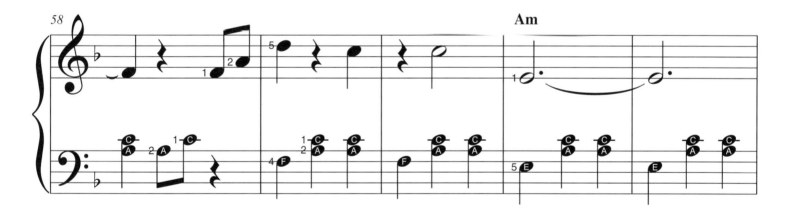

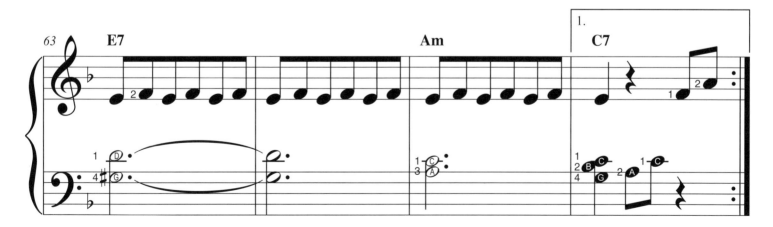

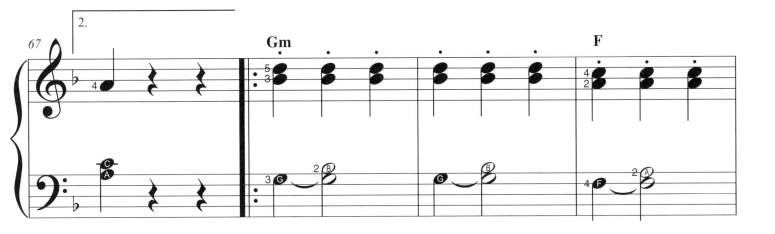

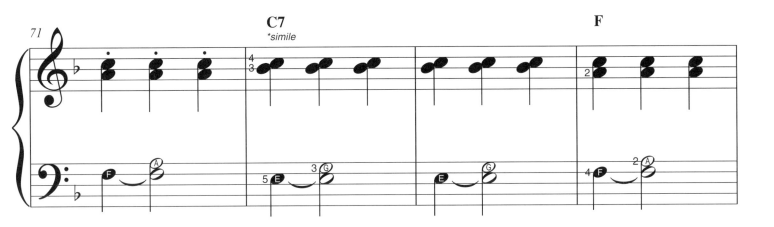

**Key: C Major**

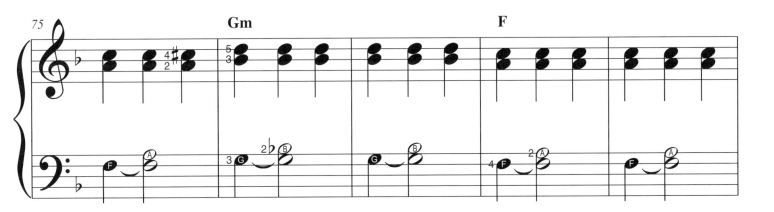

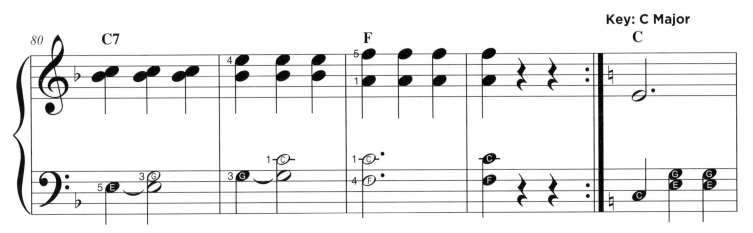

*Simile: Play in a similar manner. In this case, continue playing staccato through measure 83.

163

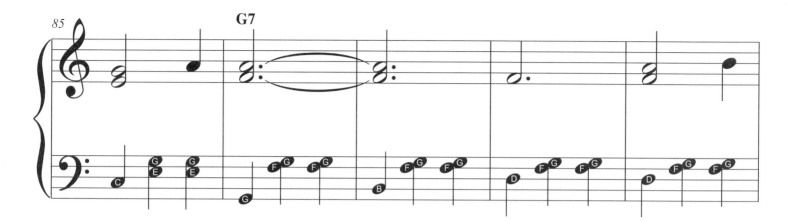

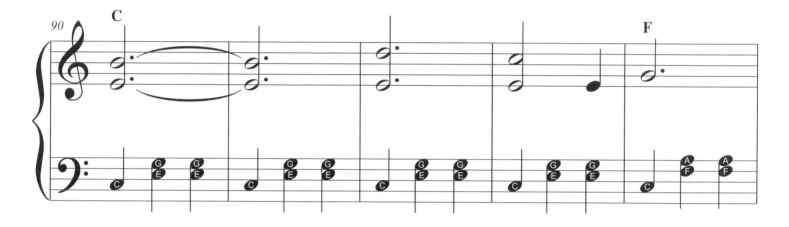

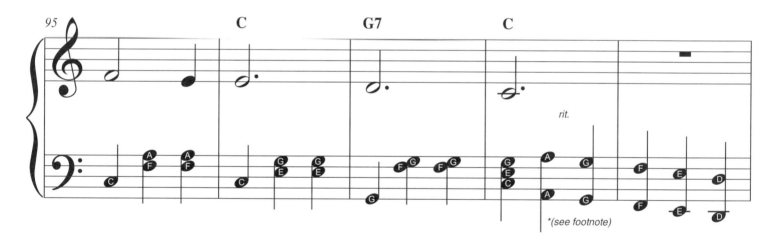

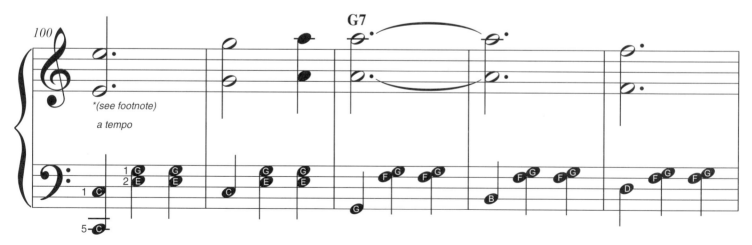

*Octaves are optional; only the top or bottom notes may be played.

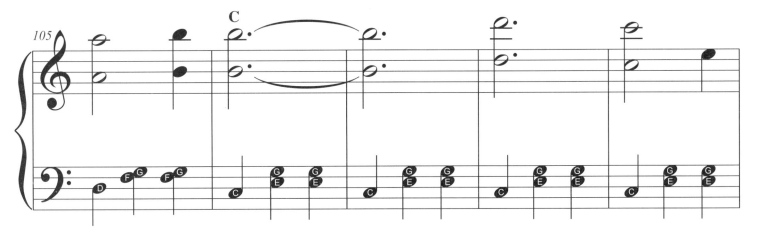

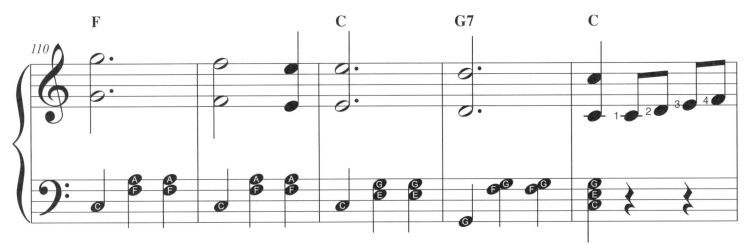

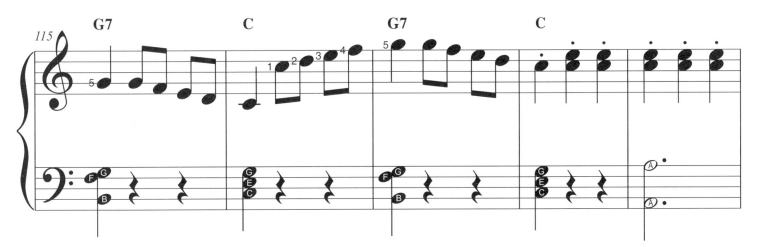

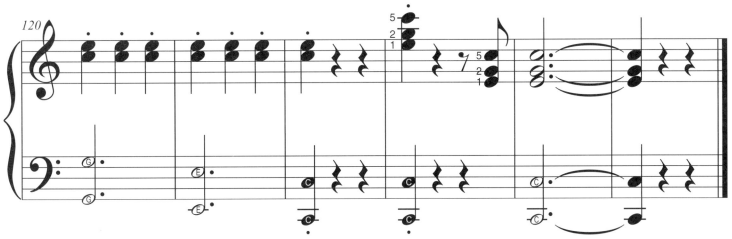

*Octaves are optional

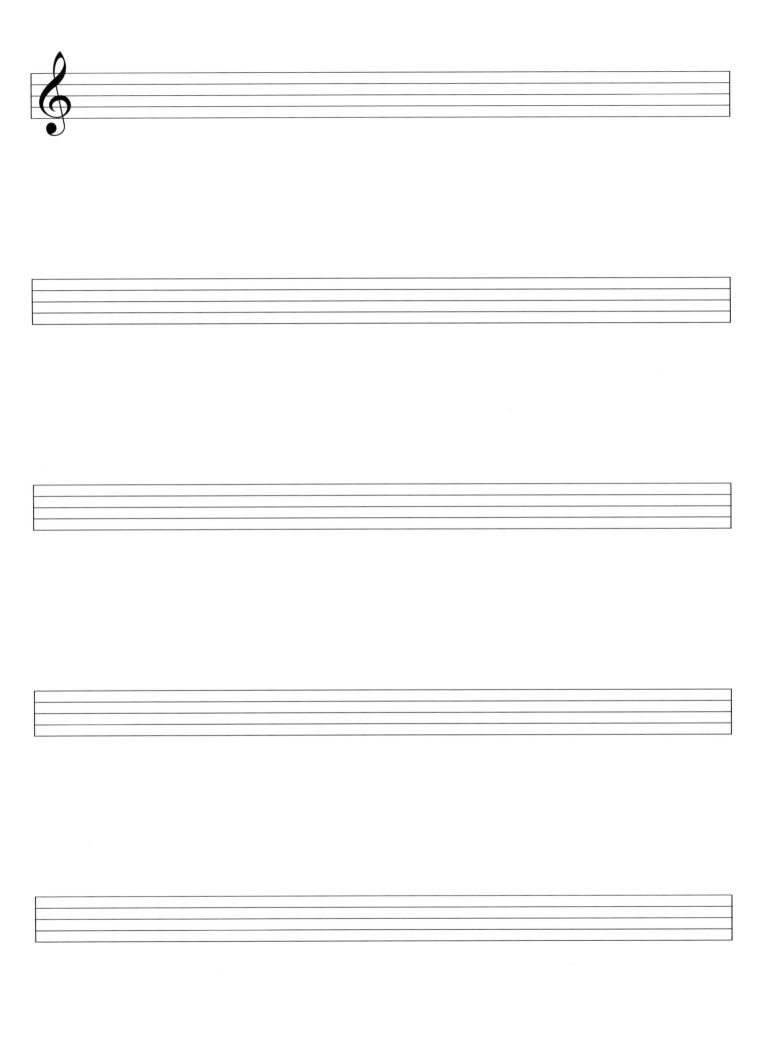

**FOR ORGANS, PIANOS & ELECTRONIC KEYBOARDS**

# E-Z PLAY® TODAY PUBLICATIONS

*The E-Z Play® Today songbook series is the shortest distance between beginning music and playing fun! Check out this list of highlights and visit www.halleonard.com for a complete listing of all volumes and songlists.*

Prices, contents, and availability subject to change without notice.